SOCIALLY CONFIDENT
in
60 SECONDS

Deborah Smith Pegues

HARVEST HOUSE PUBLISHERS
EUGENE, OREGON

Cover by Koechel Peterson & Associates, Inc., Minneapolis, Minnesota

Formerly released as *Socially Smart in 60 Seconds*

SOCIALLY CONFIDENT IN 60 SECONDS
Copyright © 2009 by Deborah Smith Pegues
Published by Harvest House Publishers
Eugene, Oregon 97402
www.harvesthousepublishers.com

Library of Congress Cataloging-in-Publication Data

Pegues, Deborah Smith,
    Socially Confident in 60 seconds / Deborah Smith Pegues.
       p. cm.
    Includes bibliographical references (p. 141).
    ISBN 978-0-7369-6229-2 (pbk.)
    ISBN 978-0-7369-6230-8 (eBook)
    1. Etiquette. I. Title.
    BJ1853.P44 2009
    395—dc22

                                                    2008020281

Printed in the United States of America

16 17 18 19 20 21 22 23 24 / BP-CD / 10 9 8 7 6 5 4 3 2

Acknowledgments

This book could not have come to fruition without the contribution of many wonderful people who desire to see the world demonstrate more civility and culture. Special appreciation goes to the members of my dream team at Harvest House Publishers: Terry Glaspey, director of acquisitions and development, for his encouragement, creativity, and always-sage advice; and Peggy Wright, Kim Moore, and the editorial staff for their diligence and commitment to producing a quality work.

Special thanks go to my friends Josie Martin and Lainie Sloane, consummate etiquette mavens, for their preliminary critique and invaluable input.

Numerous other individuals either shared their insight, social blunders, and pet peeves or they prayed for the project. They include Judge Mablean Ephraim, Paul Jackson Jr., Tyrone Potts, Kelvin and Delisa Kelley, Gene Smith, Alvin and Pamela Kelley, Redelia Fowler, Billie Rodgers, Harold and Ruth Kelley, Pamela Johnson, Kecia Ephraim, Monique Swoope, Dana Lacy, Keeley Garth, Dana Smith, Debbie Ducre, Sandra Sims Arceneaux, and Darlene Bowman.

Finally, words could never fully express my gratitude to my husband, Darnell, for his never-ending sacrifices and support to facilitate my writing efforts.

Contents

Prologue

While attending graduate school at the University of Southern California in Los Angeles, I accepted a dinner date with a fellow student who was also enrolled in the Master in Business Administration (MBA) program. The server at the slightly upscale restaurant brought us a finger bowl after our main course. Of course, we were supposed to simply dip our fingers in the small bowl of warm water and then dab them dry on the napkin. Perhaps it was the slice of lemon in the water that caused the confusion. Before I knew it, my brilliant date picked up his bowl and drank the water. I was mortified! Of course, wisdom dictated that I not react or comment, but I thought to myself, *He is in dire need of etiquette training!*

Even though we wish we could forget them, we have all made a social faux pas or two at some point in time. Unfortunately, such behavior can hinder our progress professionally, socially, and even relationally. That's why I'm writing this book. I have always been fascinated by the rules of etiquette. Growing up, I read every article and book that came my way regarding proper behavior and social graces. No one in particular encouraged my passion. I simply wanted to know how to do things right.

Immediately after graduating from the MBA program, I enrolled in the John Robert Powers finishing school. I went beyond the standard six-week course and opted for the one-year teaching curriculum. I knew that being socially polished would increase my confidence and put me at a professional advantage. The only trepidation I had about taking the course was the fear that such training would cause me to become a social perfectionist who was no fun at casual events such as picnics and ballgames. I did not want to become the etiquette cop who wrote tickets—verbal or silent—to everyone who violated proper social behavior. My fear proved to be unfounded. I learned that the whole concept of etiquette is centered on three guiding principles: consideration, convenience, and common sense. Observing proper protocol should never make others feel inferior or uncomfortable in any way.

The training at John Robert Powers was one of the best investments I've ever made. While I do not consider myself an etiquette expert, I do feel a responsibility as a Confidence Coach to provide a quick tool that will help eliminate or minimize the social insecurity and embarrassment of simply not knowing how to behave in certain situations.

As an inspirational writer, I faced somewhat of a dilemma in approaching this project. While I have a passion for teaching people how to incorporate the Bible into every aspect of their daily lives, I wrestled with the idea of trying to write an etiquette book with an inspirational twist. Further, I was concerned that potential Christian readers might consider social protocols and manners to be worldly concerns—and certainly not something that heavenly minded folks needed to spend much time pursuing. After all, using the wrong fork was not going to doom anybody to eternity with the devil and his infamous fork.

My wrestling came to a halt when I realized that etiquette is indeed the considerate, convenient, and commonsense way of relating to others. The underlying principles of such behavior come directly from the Scriptures: "Just as you want men to do to you, you also do to them likewise" (Luke 6:31). Certainly, anyone claiming to be God's child must be even more motivated to model the highest standard of social and professional manners.

I have heard some refer to social graces as "Southern hospitality." However, as I study the Bible, I realize that it is really "scriptural hospitality." God mandates certain protocols for interacting with others whether one is a Southerner or not. A former Southerner, I now live in Los Angeles, California. It is a melting pot of people of various cultures who interact with each other at warp speed—and often with great indifference. Needless to say, kindness and consideration are not the daily norm. I would love for this book to spark a movement that would abate this trend.

I have established two goals in writing this book: First, I want to instruct or remind you how to do things right so that you can gain the social confidence you need to succeed in the world. Second, I want to challenge you not only *to do things right, but to do the right thing.* Yes, doing things the proper way may enhance your career, bring you into favor with influential people, or earn you a reputation as the consummate host, but these things are secondary benefits. God has established a code of behavior that He wants to be the standard in His kingdom. I call it Kingdom Etiquette, and the rules haven't changed since the beginning of time. God always wants us to do the right thing—even when others misbehave toward us. Extending grace is the right thing to do. Columnist Thomas Sowell says,

"Politeness and consideration for others is like investing pennies and getting dollars back."

From developing a winning personality to avoiding popular pet peeves, this book will coach you to confidence in any situation. Assuming that you only have a minute or so to spare, I'll get right to the point and discuss only the essentials of each topic area. If you desire a more extensive discussion of a subject, feel free to consult any of the excellent books or websites listed in the bibliography. Now let's get started.

1

Wisdom for a Winning Personality

You could be the most polished or sophisticated person on the planet, but if people don't like you, you'll have few opportunities to interact with them. Some individuals have the kind of personality that brightens up a room, while others improve the environment by their departure.

Personality is the visible aspect of your character as it impresses others. Without a pleasing personality, achieving your personal and professional goals will be an uphill battle. This chapter is not about changing who you are or turning you into a people pleaser. It is about coming to grips with the fact that whatever you desire in life will be achieved through other people. Consequently, you must be mindful of behaviors and character traits that attract people and those that repel them.

As you read the following tips for a winning personality, consider areas where you need to shore up your interactions with others.

- Smile. Keep it genuine. Don't smile just to show off your new cosmetic veneers or caps (however, if you need them, they will be a great investment and will boost your confidence). Let your eyes smile also. A smile reflects your mental attitude, and it can affect the attitude of others.

- Listen. Be genuinely interested in other people. Try to limit the number of times you say "I" during your conversations.

- Don't interrupt—even if the person is long winded. If you need to make a point, raise your index finger slightly as if to ask for permission to speak.

- Respect other people's opinions. There is no need to argue about non-eternal matters or those that do not affect the quality of your life.

- Be quick to serve. Jesus cautioned His disciples, "The greatest among you must be a servant" (Matthew 23:11 NLT). Help others as if you were serving God Himself, because you are!

- Be generous. Don't skimp on tips to those who serve you (see chapter 13 on tipping guidelines).

- Don't be a moocher. Always pay your share—and then some.

- Be humble. Don't brag about your position, possessions, people you know, or places you've traveled. Humility tops the chart as the most admired character trait. Pride and arrogance are the most detestable.

- Don't succumb to your insecurities. Avoid putting yourself down. Know that you are adequate for every task, for your sufficiency comes from God (2 Corinthians 3:5). Confidence is a great people magnet.

- Make every effort to remember names. A person's name, to that individual, is the sweetest and most important sound in any language.

- Always make the other person feel important and

valued. Do this sincerely and without hidden motives. Booker T. Washington said, "A sure way to lift one's self up is by helping to lift someone else."

- Praise the small and large accomplishments of others, especially your employees and family members.

- Be flexible and patient when unexpected situations arise. Learning to go with the flow will increase your emotional and spiritual maturity.

- Be a peacemaker in every situation. Resist partiality or respect of persons.

- Be a team player. This will take you further than being the Lone Ranger. Don't worry about getting credit. You'll get what's yours.

- Earn the right to give constructive criticism by consistently showing concern for the other person's well-being. Always give him your input in private and after much prayer.

- Laugh. Look for the humor in negative situations. Laughter releases endorphins, the chemicals in your brain that make you feel good. Laughter is also contagious.

- Learn to be "bi-social." Know when to relax the rules of etiquette according to the situation or environment so you don't appear to be stuffy and pretentious.

- Maintain a positive attitude. Believe, according to Romans 8:28, that all things are working together for your good when you love God and are called according to His purpose.

2

Common Courtesies

Some things should go without saying. However, for those of you whose parents or guardians skimped on your home training, or who move at lightning speed and don't tend to focus on manners, I'll remind you of what indeed goes without saying.

As you read each of the common courtesies below, constantly remind yourself of the golden rule: "Whatever you want men to do to you, do also to them"(Matthew 7:12). These foundational manners will improve the quality of your life as well as the lives of those in your social or professional environment.

- Greet people. Generally, the person who enters an environment where people are already present should be the first to extend the greeting. Notwithstanding, if a person enters your space and doesn't speak first, make brownie points with God by initiating the "hello." Even when walking on the streets, speak to people with whom you make eye contact. (I know this is a Southern habit, but trust me, it works in the big city also.)

- Give people your full attention when meeting with them. This is not the time to complete mindless busy work (organizing your desk, etc.) to redeem the time.

- Say "thank you" whenever anybody extends any kindness or courtesy to you or does anything to ensure your comfort or well-being. This includes family members who take out the trash, husbands who are financially responsible, wives who make dinner, pastors who deliver a great message, employees who finish a report on time, the waiter who brings your food, your gardener, the UPS delivery person, or anyone else who enhances your existence or adds value to your life.

- Say "please" when requesting anything from anybody, even if you ask your child to close the door. You can't bark orders at folks and expect them to have warm fuzzy feelings toward you.

- Say "excuse me" when you interrupt, inconvenience, annoy, or cause a person any kind of discomfort or irritation (such as when you accidentally slurp when sucking through a straw).

- Don't stare at people. Be sure to pass this lesson on to your children. It makes people uncomfortable.

- Don't ignore disabled people when in a social setting. Talk to them. (But do not ask how they became disabled.) Engage in the same type of small talk as you would toward nonphysically challenged persons.

- Don't tell an overweight person that she is fat. This is not news to her. Do not comment on someone's weight gain in the presence of a weight-challenged person.

- Knock before you open a closed door. Wait for permission to enter even when it relates to your teenager.

- R.S.V.P. is an abbreviation of the French phrase

"répondez s'il vous plaît." It means to reply to an invitation—whether you plan to attend or not. Unless the invitation says "and guest" after your name, it is for you only. Do not add the names of people you would like to invite. If in doubt, call the host and obtain clarity. Once you have confirmed your attendance, show up or you'll look flaky and irresponsible for causing the host to incur unnecessary costs.

- Don't discipline your children in public. It's usually unnecessary if done at home. People are stressed enough without watching the drama of a rambunctious rebel and a powerless parent.

- Respect your elders. Go out of your way to assist an older person.

- Hold the door open for those following behind you.

- Walk to the right (in the United States) on sidewalks. If walking with another person, form a single line when you meet someone coming in the opposite direction.

- Let other people exit the elevator before you step on. Offer to press the respective floor numbers for others if you're nearest to the floor control panel. Do not reach across someone to press your floor number. Ask the person near the panel to do it for you.

- Don't call someone's house late at night unless it's an emergency. Find out what he considers "late" and honor his time boundary.

- If you call a wrong number, say "I'm sorry. Wrong number" rather than just hanging up the phone.

- Identify yourself when you call someone. "Hello, this is

Barbara Brown from the office. May I speak to John?" (or "Mr. Smith" if you are not on a first name basis with John). Also, if calling a married couple's house and the spouse of the opposite sex answers the phone, be respectful and fully identify the nature of your call: "Hello, Mrs. Smith. This is Donna Davis from the office. We need Mr. Smith's urgent input on a problem. Is he available to take my call?" Don't say: "Mrs. Smith, I need to speak with John."

- Apologize when you keep people waiting—and don't make it a habit.

- Call before you pay a visit to someone's home.

3

Money Manners

How much did you pay for that car?" the inquisitive passerby asked as I was putting coins into the parking meter. "A lot!" I responded, trying to hide my annoyance while at the same time attempting to be gracious. Obviously, he didn't know that such a question was in poor taste and frankly none of his business. While the Scriptures declare "money answereth all things" (Ecclesiastes 10:19 KJV), we have no obligation to answer all the things people want to know about our money matters.

It's no secret that we live in a materialistic society, and money issues are often at the forefront. It is our secret, however, as to how much we earn, pay for our necessities or toys, or how much we invest. However, just in case you're in doubt about how far you can poke into someone's affairs or how to respond when people practice bad money manners, here's the scoop.

Personal Situations

- Develop a few pat (even lighthearted) answers to nosey questions regarding how much anything costs: "Under a million dollars!" "That's confidential." "Are you planning to buy one?" "Why don't I give you the seller's

contact information and you can work out the details."
"It's a secret. I'll have to shoot you if I tell you."

- It is okay to share bargain-price information with close friends. "Can you believe I only paid $20 for these boots?" Share the deals.

- Never brag about the high cost or brand name of anything. This is a glaring display of low self-esteem and the need for validation and acceptance.

- Money often separates friends, so try to never ask a friend for a loan. If you must ask due to an emergency, voluntarily agree to sign an official promissory note that sets forth a due date and the amount of interest, if any, to be paid. Consider that your friend will lose interest on these funds while they are in your possession. If for reasons beyond your control you will not be able to honor the due date, advise your friend right away. If you are the lender, ask as many detailed questions as necessary to satisfy yourself that a true emergency exists. Feel free to say no—especially if the borrower is financially irresponsible. When will he ever learn his lesson if you continue to be his safety net?

- It is not proper to ask for a loan from someone who is a friend of your close friend or relative—even if you know she has the money. You will appear to be a taker or opportunist for sure since you do not have a close relationship with that person.

- Don't feel obligated to reciprocate the value of a gift from a friend or relative. If, because of your limited funds, you cannot afford or don't wish to spend a similar amount that was spent on you, buy what you feel the person would use or enjoy. If the recipient is shallow enough to mention the disparity in the value of your gift versus his, kindly (maybe lightheartedly) reply, "I didn't realize we were keeping score. You win."

- It is tacky to plan your birthday party and then instruct guests to plan on decorating a "money tree" in lieu of gifts. This is like calling somebody up and saying, "Send me some money."

- If you organize a celebration for a friend, consider everybody's budget when selecting the restaurant. Provide the menu price range when possible and also inform the participants ahead of time if you expect them to chip in more for the honoree's meal and group gift. Nothing is more embarrassing than for a guest to show up with a specific amount of money and then be hit with twice the expected cost. If you are the struggling guest, you must always expect to share the cost of the honoree's meal, so plan for it or decline the invitation if you can't swing it.

- If you must talk money, keep it generic. Stick to discussing prices for gasoline, housing, college tuition, and so on.

Business Situations

- Never discuss your salary, raise, bonus, or perks with anyone at work except your boss and the Human Resources department. You may create a morale problem for others—or yourself—if you find out that you are at the bottom of the pay scale.

- If someone asks you how much you make, respond, "Not as much as I dream about making."

4

Confident Dining

A person's lack of social or professional polish will often be most noticeable in the dining arena. There are quite a few guidelines that you need to be aware of if you want to claim "savvy diner" status:

Napkin Etiquette

- Place your napkin on your lap as soon as you are seated or as soon as your host does so. Your napkin will be located:

    - on your left (to the left of or under your fork)
    - on your plate
    - in your glass, which is on your right at the tip of your knife

- If someone unknowingly takes your napkin, do not point it out, make a big deal of it, or explain the rules of napkin etiquette. Graciously ask, "Could you pass me that napkin over there, please?"

- If it is a large dinner napkin, don't unfold it completely. Use it half folded in a triangle. Lunch-sized napkins may be used fully unfolded.

- Do not turn your napkin into a bib by tucking it in the neck of your collar. If eating lobster, the restaurant will provide a special bib for you.

- Do not use the napkin as you would a tissue (for example, for blowing your nose). Use a handkerchief or tissue.

- If you must leave the table during the meal, place your napkin on your chair. This keeps others from having to look at a soiled napkin.

- At the end of the meal, place your unfolded napkin on the table to the left of your plate. This will alert your waiter that you are finished eating.

Glassware/Drinking Etiquette

- Water glasses are placed at the tip of the knife. All other glasses are placed to the right of the water glass.

- Do not drink with food in your mouth. The sight of food particles in a glass is disgusting.

- If a toast is given, the honoree never takes a drink. It is equivalent to applauding himself.

Eating Etiquette

- Begin eating when your host starts. It is usually courteous to wait until all others at the table have been served, but if you have ordered a soufflé or dish that cools in seconds, wait until the diners on either side of you have been served before you dig in. If everyone has been served except you, ask them to go ahead to keep their food from getting cold.

- Know your place setting. One expert suggests you remember BMW: bread on the left, meal in the middle, and water on the right. Your forks are on the left. Your knife is on the right with the cutting edge turned toward the plate. The spoons are to the right of the knive, the larger one being for the soup. The fork and/or spoon at the top of the plate is for dessert. You can't go wrong if you simply start with the outer utensils and work your way in.

- Select your bread roll from the breadbasket with your hand and place it on your bread plate, located on your left above the fork. (I once saw someone select a roll by spearing it with his fork in a quick and jerky fashion.) If the supply of butter is served via a community dish rather than in individual pats, use the knife that accompanies the dish to transfer an adequate amount of butter to your bread-and-butter plate.

- Do not cut your bread roll in half; break and butter only one bite at a time. Always use the butter knife from your butter plate or your dinner knife to butter your bread rather than the one that accompanies the community butter dish.

- Do not cut up all your food at once like a child. Cut and eat only one bite at a time.

- You may cut your lettuce if it is not served in bite-sized pieces.

- If the waiter takes away your knife, ask for another one.

- In a casual social situation, certain foods—asparagus, shrimp cocktail with the tail on, french fries, fried chicken, ribs—may be eaten with your fingers. However, if asparagus is served as a side dish, use your knife. When eating meat that has a bone (ribs, chicken) cut what you can off the bone, but don't chew on the bone in public.

- When someone asks you to pass the salt or the pepper, pass both together.

- Sit up straight. Do not hunch over your plate.

- Bring your food up to your mouth rather than bending over and meeting it halfway or near your plate.

- Do not smack, slurp, suck your teeth, or make any noises with your mouth.

- If you drop a utensil on the floor, do not pick it up. Notify the waiter, and he'll bring you a clean one.

- At no time should used silverware be placed on the table.

- Conceal empty sugar packets neatly under your coffee or tea saucer. Put a used tea bag on the side of the saucer if no teapot is available.

- When eating soup, spoon the soup away from you (with a soupspoon) and sip from the side of the spoon; do not put the entire bowl of the spoon in your mouth. Tilt the soup bowl away from you to get the last spoonful.

- Do not talk or laugh with food in your mouth.

- Do not chew your ice. It's annoying to most people.

- Do not bang your silverware on the plate as you eat.

- Don't be a diet bore by discussing calories, the perils of eating meat, or any other foods matters that cast a negative light on the food choices of fellow diners.

At the End of the Meal

- Ladies, when eating out, do not stack the dirty plates at the end of the meal. Thanks, but you're off duty right now.

- When finished, place your fork and knife close together across your plate diagonally at the "10 'til 4" position; fork on the left, facing upward; knife parallel to it with the cutting edge facing the fork.  This tells the waiter you have taken your last bite.

- The appropriate tip is 15 to 20 percent of the bill before taxes. However, if your party lingers at a table longer than a normal meal cycle, consider your waiter's lost tip opportunity and leave a double tip.

- At a buffet, if a waiter serves you in any manner (brings

water, removes excess dishes, etc.), leave him at least 10 percent of the bill and no less than $1 to $2 per person.

- If you are going to use a toothpick, do so in the restroom or the car and not in public. Never use dental floss or its equivalent in public.

5

Business Dining and Entertaining

———————

Business manners seem to have become a hot topic in recent years. Image consultants cite many instances of strained client relations, missed opportunities, and pure embarrassment caused by a lack of social and professional savvy in corporate representatives.

Manners and professional polish are critical to your success in business. Your socials skills at the table may be the final factor in the decision to hire or promote you, or to expose you to greater opportunities. Further, a key client may judge your firm by how well the executives handle themselves in the area of dining and entertaining.

Let's take a quick look at some essentials.

Dining

In addition to the regular rules for dining discussed in chapter 4, additional guidelines and caveats are in order for business meals. This is where dining savvy literally pays off.

- When hosting a business meal, ask your guest if she prefers a certain restaurant. If she has no preference, choose an establishment where you are familiar with the quality of the food, ambiance, and service. Ideally, the staff would also be familiar with you. It's quite impressive when the restaurant host greets you by name. "Hello, Ms. Brown. Come this way, please."

- Always confirm your appointment with the guest the day before as well as the location. I've heard horror stories ranging from being at the wrong location of a chain restaurant to the appointment being a week later.

- Plan to arrive ten minutes or so before your reservation to make sure your table is in a favorable spot—away from the door, kitchen, or other noisy, high-traffic areas.

- If you're trying to impress someone, avoid difficult-to-eat food, such as crab legs, French onion soup, lobster, spaghetti, or a mile-high messy sandwich. Stick with simple fare.

- Don't ask to taste someone's food when dining with clients, special guests, or superiors.

- Wait until the meal is completed before starting business talk. This will allow you to establish rapport as well as minimize disruptions from the waitstaff.

- If the meeting will require you to review documents that will need to be spread out, consider having the meeting at your or his office and plan to have lunch afterward. Reviewing only a page or two at the table is acceptable.

- Some etiquette experts suggest that you arrange to pay for the meal ahead of time by giving the waiter your credit card prior to the guest's arrival. With rising identify thefts and credit card fraud, you may not want your card out of sight very long—even at an upscale restaurant. If you prefer, you may pay in the presence of your guest. Just quickly review the bill and present your card. If you discover an error on the bill, point it out discreetly. Simply say to the waiter, "Would you kindly recheck this item, please?"

- Don't ask for a doggie bag (unless you and the guest are quite familiar with each other and she has done so before). You'll look as though you're trying to get maximum personal mileage out of a free meal.

Business Entertaining

Occasionally you may decide that a special outing at a restaurant or even your home would be an effective way to say thanks or to strengthen business relationships. The protocols of business entertaining are similar to personal entertaining with a few nuances. The items set forth below are the least that you should do.

- If the event is held after hours, consider including spouses and significant others as you are using their personal time.

- If hosting in your home, it is best to hire help for a few hours. Be sure to explain ahead of time to those assisting you your druthers and personal quirks in terms of food service, interacting with guests, timely removal of cocktail dishes, etc. A preprinted list of dos and don'ts may be helpful to avoid frustrations and embarrassment.

- Your primary responsibility when hosting is to greet your guests and to make sure that they meet others and have a good time in general.

- Depending on the size of the gathering and the

familiarity of the group with each other, you might consider using name badges. Assign someone the responsibility of making sure everyone is wearing one, except the guest of honor (if applicable)—with whom everyone should be familiar.

- Prepare brief remarks to make near the end of the event to thank the guests and to inform them of any positive news, decisions, or information.

6

Making Introductions

Introductions are critical in a social or business environment as they open the door for people to communicate with each other. Many people dread introducing others because the guidelines for doing so can be confusing. The general rule for making introductions is to say the name of the person whom you desire to give the most honor or respect *first*. You may simply say, "Ms. More Prominent, I'd like to introduce (or, "I'd like you to meet") Ms. Less Prominent." Note that Less Prominent is always *presented* to More Prominent. The guidelines for who is more or less prominent differ in social versus business situations. In social settings, *age* and *gender* are the key factors in determining who is to be given the highest honor. In the business world, *rank* and *authority* determine who has more prominence.

Social Introductions:

More Prominent (Say this person's name first)	Less Prominent (One being presented)
Elected Official	Nonofficial person
Adults	Younger Adults/Children
Women	Men
Elderly Woman	*Everybody* except the President
Unfamiliar Guest	Host/Hostess
Guest of Honor	Other Guests
Pastors/Priests	Lay People
Professors	Parents/Students
Doctors	Patients
Friends	Siblings/Relatives

Business Introductions:

More Prominent (Say this person's name first)	Less Prominent (One being presented)
CEO	Jr. Executives and Staff
Customer/Client	CEO (that's right!) and Staff
Elected Official	CEO
Peer in another company	Peer in your company

- Be sure to clearly articulate each person's full name so all parties can grasp it.

- More Prominent should extend his or her hand for a good, firm (but not crushing) handshake to Less Prominent. The handshake should involve the entire hand with the web of each party's thumbs becoming one unit. Avoid limp, fingertips only handshakes. Women especially consider such handshakes distasteful.

- As you present Less Prominent to More Prominent, it is important to put the conversational ball in motion by explaining who they are, your relationship to them, their employment, and common interests, hobbies, or other pertinent information. For example, "Joan, I'd like you to meet my brother, Harry Gray. Harry, this is Joan Brown. She is the author of *Trapped*, the book I told you about the other day."

- More Prominent acknowledges the introduction by saying, "It's nice to meet you, Less Prominent" or, "How do you do, Less Prominent?" Saying the name immediately will help you to remember it. Of course, it is essential to accompany the handshake with good eye contact and a genuine smile.

- Everybody should stand during an introduction (except the elderly or disabled). Yes, I know that according to nineteenth-century etiquette a woman can remain seated, but if you are on the corporate fast track, why bring extra attention to the gender difference? Of course, if you are seated in the middle in a restaurant booth with diners on both sides, let common sense prevail.

- One final word of caution: Do not get too familiar with More Prominent by calling him by his first name without his telling you to do so. If people of equal age and rank are introduced, they may use each other's first name immediately after being introduced.

7

Making Small Talk

You may have attended social or business gatherings in the past and found it frightening, or at the least uncomfortable, to strike up a conversation with total strangers. If you're not a person with the gift of gab, don't despair. The thing to remember is not so much what *you* say, but what you get others to say. Here is a fail-safe rule: Get people to talk about their favorite subject—themselves! How do you do this? By asking open-ended questions that require more than a yes or no response. Of course, you'll also need to arm yourself with a little bit of conversational fodder by being prepared to talk about a few current news stories. You may find it helpful to listen to an all-news radio station, read the opinion section of the newspaper, or check a headline news site on the Internet, such as news.yahoo .com or www.time.com.

Try setting a goal of talking to five or more unfamiliar people during the course of the event. If you implement the tips below, you should come away with others hailing you as a good conversationalist.

- Smile. Look approachable.
- Remind yourself that you belong at the event. Envision

yourself as the missing piece in the social puzzle. The gathering would not be complete without you.

- Introduce yourself—slowly articulating your full name—to anybody who seems interesting. Forget about their rank. Everybody rates!

- If the spelling of your name is odd and you're not wearing a nametag, you might want to spell it—not that you expect anybody to remember it, but this can be a great conversation starter. When introducing yourself, be sure to include helpful information that will allow the person to ask you follow-up questions.

"Hello, I'm John Brown. I'm a sales manager with X company."

"Hi, I'm Helen Smith. I'm the aunt of the bride."

- When you're introduced to someone, ask questions that show your interest. "That's a unique last name. What's its origin?" "What inspired you to go into your line of business?" "What is your relationship to the bride and groom?"

- Ask about a current news event: "Did you catch that story about the woman who...?" Or a recent sporting event, "Was that an awesome Super Bowl game or what?"

- Avoid controversial topics such as politics, religion, race, sexual orientation, and so forth. However, if you get pulled into such a discussion, respect the opinion of others and don't attempt to make them agree with your point of view. Remember, a dissenting opinion is not a personal attack, and it will not affect the quality of your life.

- Don't get too personal by asking about someone's weight, salary, price of clothing/possessions, or other private information.

- Refrain from discussing your therapist or the details of your recent illness or surgery.

- Remember that this is "small" talk. Don't bore your listener with long, technical dialogue.

- Give the person you're talking to your full attention. Don't let your eyes dart around the room as if looking for a more interesting individual.

- Move on gracefully to the next person. Simply extend your hand for a handshake and use an exit line such as, "It's been nice talking to you" or "I wish you the best on your project."

8

Networking

If you want to succeed, you must be willing to interact with people who can help you—and vice versa. Don't assume that everyone will beat a path to your door to secure your products or services with no effort on your part. God works through people, and that means networking.

When Joseph was thrown into prison in the land of Egypt, the connection he made with Pharaoh's cupbearer, a fellow prisoner, proved mutually beneficial. When the cupbearer asked Joseph to interpret his troublesome dream, he did so. He then implored the cupbearer to speak to Pharaoh on his behalf once he got out of prison: "When all goes well with you, remember me and show me kindness; mention me to Pharaoh and get me out of this prison" (Genesis 40:14 NIV). Even though the cupbearer forgot about him (verse 23), he remembered him two years later at the time God knew would be most beneficial. Pharaoh had a dream of impending economic turmoil but did not know what to make of it. Upon the cupbearer's recommendation, he called Joseph in to interpret the dream. Not only did Joseph explain the dream, he also presented the perfect economic strategy to deal with the inevitable famine. Because his wisdom and skill for the job were so evident, Pharaoh made him second-in-command. Joseph became a wealthy and famous man in a country where he had been a captive (Genesis 41). Talk about an overnight success!

You never know how a person you meet will impact your destiny. Reach out with an intent to serve, and see where that will take you.

The guidelines below will help you to put your best networking foot forward and inspire others to interact with you—or on your behalf.

- Show up. Those with outgoing personalities relish opportunities to network with people great and small. However, the fact that you may be shy is no reason to shy away from such opportunities. The only way to overcome a fear is to just do it.

- If name tags are available, they are to be worn on the right, so that when you shake a person's right hand, your eyes naturally stay focused on his right side and vice versa.

- Introduce yourself (see the previous chapter).

- When you are introduced to someone, say the person's name immediately and use it at least a couple of times during your conversation to reinforce it in your memory. My husband remembers best by associating the person's name with someone he knows who has the same name. I prefer to associate the name with something unusual or bizarre. For example: For Angela Bassett, I would envision an angel leaning over a bassinet. Memory experts recommend both methods. It all depends on what works for you.

- Introduce people to others whom you feel would benefit

by knowing them. If you forget one of their names, just say so. "I'm sorry, but I'm having a bit of brain drain. Tell me your name again."

- Make appropriate small talk (again, refer to chapter 7 for guidelines).

- Place a supply of business cards in a pocket of your jacket or purse for quick retrieval when someone asks for one, but don't offer it until asked. Make sure your cards are crisp, clean, and free of notes written on the back.

- If someone did not bring his business card but expresses a desire for you to contact him later, simply write his information on the back of one of your cards. Immediately put an "X" or other distinguishing mark on the front of the card to remind you not to give it out because of the information on the back. A small notepad may also be used, but you'll want to avoid the appearance of being a reporter doing research for a story.

- Always keep tiny breath mints handy. Put a few in your pocket (not the one where the business cards are!) for quick and subtle access. Breath spray works also, but it can sometimes leaving you smelling like a mint factory, and it's hard to use without being noticed because it also has sound effects.

- Do not monopolize the attention of the special guest. Consider that others (especially if they are waiting in line) would like a few minutes of her time also. Move on after a minute or so—or less. (I stood in line once and waited for more than ten minutes during a break to say hello to a popular psychologist who was the guest speaker. The man ahead of me used all of the time. I was upset with him for being so inconsiderate—and with the speaker for tolerating it. The speaker could have simply said, "It was nice talking to you, Charlie. I'm going to say hello to a few others now.")

- Follow up immediately on your promise to provide information, product samples, etc. Be realistic on the time frame when promising. Give yourself a week rather than "tomorrow." Your integrity is at stake. God welcomes into His presence those who "keep their promises even when it hurts" (Psalm 15:4 NLT).

- At a cocktail reception, don't overdo it on the food. Avoid taking large mouthfuls, which slow you down in responding to questions directed to you.

- Hold your glass in your left hand, and keep your right hand dry for handshaking. Stemmed glasses should be held by the stem.

- Try to bring closure to your conversations before moving on to the next person. Don't just ease into oblivion when the person looks away or someone else distracts him. Offer a handshake and a parting remark. "It was great talking to you. I wish you success on your project" or "I wish you the best."

9

Office Etiquette

The annual compensation for the average American worker is based on 2080 hours per year (fifty-two 40-hour weeks). When you spend that much time with a group of people, you would be wise to learn how to relate to them in a mutually beneficial manner. You must focus on helping the company to achieve its objectives while fulfilling your financial and career goals.

Whether at work or at home, all human interactions are best governed by spoken and unspoken rules of conduct. The guidelines below represent foundational considerations and boundaries that should maximize productivity while allowing for balanced, professional relationships.

- Remember that your employer's primary objective is to produce a quality product or service. Despite the fact that birthdays may be celebrated, you should not expect the office to be a place where you get your relational or emotional needs (for appreciation, affirmation, etc.) met. Lower your expectation in this area.

- Be clear and consistent with your conversational boundaries. Don't divulge any personal information you do not want repeated. Likewise, do not pry into the affairs of others.

- If you need to put someone on hold or transfer a call to someone else, advise the caller before you do so. Otherwise, you come across as an inconsiderate employee devoid of personality.

- Don't be the local news anchor for the company's rumor mill. Gossip detracts from your professionalism, diminishes your integrity, and derails you from the fast track. You will also be wise to avoid other gossips. "Do not be misled: 'Bad company corrupts good character'" (1 Corinthians 15:33 NIV).

- Watch the volume at which you speak—especially if you share an office or work in a cubicle. This is one of the most frequent gripes of office workers. Show your sensitivity to those around you by asking them if your volume is disruptive to their productivity.

- Don't be a boss basher. One day you may be the boss.

- Don't be a company basher. If the company is so bad, why are you still working there? Don't have any other options? Either develop your exit strategy or stop complaining.

- Don't be either a clock-watcher or feel obligated to be the last one out the door. Seek balance.

- If you are a supervisor, be as personable as you can with your subordinates while maintaining professionalism. Resist becoming chummy or too familiar with a staff person (especially of the opposite sex). Such behavior will demoralize the other staff members and hinder your effectiveness.

- Don't use terms of endearment such as "dear," "sweetheart," or "honey" when addressing anybody in the workplace. It could subject you to sexual harassment charges—plus it's annoying in general and unprofessional.

- Feel free to say no to the endless solicitations to buy candy, magazine subscriptions, and other fund-raising products on behalf of coworkers' kids. Do what you can afford.

- Don't warm strong-smelling foods in the microwave oven. (Years ago I attempted to heat a fish entrée and obviously left it in too long. One of the executives gave me a serious tongue-lashing. It was a long time before I ate fish anywhere after that.)

- Don't hog the company refrigerator. At the most, keep only a bottle of dressing in it for a week at a time. Suppose that everyone stored as much as you. How would that work for you?

- Maintain a tidy work space. Imagine the impression you give of your company—and yourself—when others encounter your chaos. It smacks of disorganization and poor planning. (One of my old bosses taught me a system in which I used a file folder for each of my pending projects and stacked them in a desktop file holder. Rather than flipping through endless papers, I was able to immediately pull the needed folder simply by looking at the label. He also stressed the importance of working on one thing at a time. It's still a challenge to work with only one folder on my desk, but when I do, I feel less stressed and much more in control.)

- Embrace and celebrate personality differences in the workplace. I once had five different ethnic groups on my staff of ten. From time to time, at our staff meetings, I would ask them to share with us their unique cultural differences and sensitivities. We all learned a lot and became a really close-knit group. We loved it when the Filipino woman brought in native dishes for us on her birthday. It's their custom to do so.

- When you have a conflict with a coworker, don't go silent or ballistic. Determine to be a peacemaker and confront the issues personally, promptly, privately, and peacefully. Yelling or becoming emotional is unprofessional and is a strong indication of emotional and relational immaturity. Remember, the person who controls his emotions will produce the most rational argument and gain the greatest respect. When emotions go up, rational thinking goes down—just like a seesaw. "A person without self-control is like a city with broken-down walls" (Proverbs 25:28 NLT).

- Be sure to obtain your supervisor's approval to use headphones or this may come up during your annual review. Some employees find headphones beneficial when doing work (such as data entry) that requires minimal concentration.

- Skip the personal radio. Don't assume everyone shares your taste in music. Even with the volume turned down low, it may still impact the efficiency of those within earshot. (When I worked at a religious nonprofit, one of my employees was offended by the music from the jazz station listened to by her coworker on her personal radio. Their work was somewhat monotonous, so we compromised by allowing the use of earphones.)

10

Meeting Manners and Protocols

Whether you are chairing or participating in a meeting in a social, religious, or professional setting, certain courtesies and protocols should be observed to assure the effectiveness of the outcome. Follow these guidelines for a productive meeting.

Your Behavior as the Chair

- If possible, send a notice to all participants a few days ahead of time with a proposed agenda (or at least a good description of the nature of the meeting). Advise them of the start time and an estimate of the expected duration of the meeting. Include in the notice the names of all invited participants. To be safe and to avoid ruffling feathers, ask invitees to advise you immediately of the names of other key players who may have inadvertently been omitted from the list.

- Refrain from wearing anything distracting, such as gaudy rings, clanging bracelets, swinging earrings, plunging necklines, etc. (Once during a presentation I forgot to remove a four-inch silver hair clip that was temporarily holding my bangs in place. At the break, a fellow employee asked me if I knew it was there. Talk about embarrassment!)

- Appoint a person to record the minutes of the meeting.

- Start on time. Remember, what you tolerate establishes a precedent. Don't let your actions imply that tardiness is acceptable.

- Ask if anyone desires to add any other discussion to the agenda. If the agenda is full, promise to include the item in the next meeting's agenda.

- Stay focused on the agenda. Don't ramble or engage in a self-promoting discourse. Do not allow others to go down irrelevant rabbit trails that lead to nowhere. Kindly say, "I'm going to keep my commitment to end the meeting at the scheduled time, so we need to stay focused on the matter at hand."

- Do not allow the meeting to deteriorate into sidebar conversations. A statement such as, "I need everyone's attention" or "Do you guys care to share your concern with the group?" should be sufficient to get the sidebar spoilers to refocus on the group.

- When conducting a brainstorming session, don't reject any idea as unacceptable. Simply respond, "That's an idea" or "I'd like to review the details later on how to implement your suggestion." This will keep people inspired to give input. (I was in a brainstorming meeting once in which the chair kept evaluating or rejecting the ideas put forth. After about the third rejection, everyone clammed up. Galatians 6:1 (KJV) immediately came to my mind. "If a man be overtaken in a fault, ye which are

spiritual, restore such an one in the spirit of meekness."
I did just that. I gently told him the impact his actions
had on the participants. I am happy to report that at the
next meeting, not one idea was rejected.)

- Familiarize yourself with Roberts Rules of Order (www
  .robertsrules.org) for the how-tos of conducting constructive and democratic meetings involving motions,
  voting, etc.

- Assign action items to appropriate individuals for
  follow-up.

- Obtain a consensus on the most convenient time to
  schedule the next meeting.

- Have the meeting recorder send copies of the minutes
  to all participants within a couple of days of the meeting. Be sure to keep the minutes brief. Nothing is more
  time wasting than having to wade through a blow-by-
  blow account of a meeting in search of the bottom line.
  Highlights of the discussion and motions passed are
  sufficient.

- End the meeting on time. Don't earn a reputation for
  conducting long, boring meetings.

Your Behavior as a Participant

- Arrive on time. Apologize when you are late to a meeting, and don't make tardiness a habit.

- Silence your cell phone.

- Bring your business cards if unfamiliar parties will be
  attending the meeting.

- Avoid engaging in sidebar conversations with fellow

participants. This is rude and distracting. If something is worth discussing, ask the chair to allow you to speak.

- Be prepared to take notes and to participate. Don't assume the meeting will be a waste of time.

- Maintain a positive attitude. Negativity is contagious and thwarts effectiveness.

- Be mindful of engaging in annoying and distracting behavior, such as clicking a ballpoint pen, drumming on the table with your fingers, tapping your foot, slurping coffee or tea, or flipping through your notes/papers.

- Don't be a yes man or woman by simply going along with whatever your superiors or senior executives suggest—especially when you know that you have a viable alternative to what is on the table. Respectfully ask, "Could we also consider...?"

- If you become drowsy, quietly excuse yourself and take a quick coffee/restroom break. I've seen some meeting participants stand in the back of the room for a spell until they feel revived. Better than nodding off and running the risk of snoring.

- Respect the input of others by not interrupting them. Raise your hand to ask a question rather than just blurting it out.

- Get straight to the point when asking questions or making comments. Don't prolong the meeting with trivia or unnecessary war stories.

- Women, don't sabotage your credibility by being tentative in putting forth your ideas or suggestions. Example: "Well, this may not be a good idea, but..."

- If you attend a recurring meeting with the same participants, honor the established seating pattern. (I was on a seven-person board once and, just like homing pigeons, everyone always returned to "his" seat at each monthly meeting. Occasionally, we'd have a special guest who would arrive early and upset the whole seating order.) If someone takes "your" seat; don't sweat it...flow... flow...flow.

- Refrain from upstaging or correcting your boss. If a matter is critical, simply ask a clarifying question. Always make your boss look good in the presence of others. This will earn you great career mileage!

11

Job Interview Etiquette

Interviewing can be nerve-racking, as your every action and word are under the microscope. Before you blow your opportunity to make a good first impression, consider the essential points of etiquette below before, during, and after the interview.

Before the Interview

- Learn as much as you can about the company (via website, annual report, etc.) and a little about what distinguishes it from its competitors (if relevant).

- Understand the nature of the advertised job.

- Be honest with yourself as to why you are seeking employment with the particular company. Do you just need to earn a paycheck or is it part of your career strategy?

- Rehearse answers to potentially difficult questions regarding your long-term goals, your people skills, etc.

- Find out about the company's interviewing process (preliminary versus follow-up interviews).

- Select attire appropriate for the industry. Dress for success by selecting an outfit a step above the proposed job. Women should wear a conservative suit or dress with a jacket, hosiery, sensible shoes for touring the facility if necessary, moderate makeup, minimal jewelry, a hairstyle that doesn't cover the eyes, short- to medium-length nails, and just a hint of perfume. Short, tight, or suggestive clothing may cost you the job. Men should wear a conservative suit-and-tie combo with a light-colored shirt, shined shoes with dark socks, minimum facial hair, and clean trimmed nails.

- Put your résumé, notepad, and pen in a nice portfolio. These are available at your local office supply store.

- Bring an extra copy or two of your résumé. They often get misplaced by the various people who may interview you.

- Silence your cell phone.

- Arrive early. Plan to be outside the interviewer's office no later than ten minutes prior to the scheduled interview.

The Interview

- Offer the interviewer a firm handshake and a pleasant smile while maintaining good eye contact.

- Do not take a seat until he instructs you to do so.

- Do not complain about any woes of the day (traffic, rain, etc.).

- Do not put your briefcase or portfolio on the interviewer's desk.

- Don't try to get chummy with the interviewer. Keep your tone friendly but professional.

- Answer the specific question and don't bore the interviewer with irrelevant details.

- Don't look away when a question is asked. It makes you look deceitful. Maintain eye contact when answering.

- Never use profanity. Remember, you're being judged on every action.

- Don't bad-mouth or criticize your current (or previous) employer. When asked why you're pursuing the job, talk about career goals instead.

- Don't be either too cocky or too modest. Highlight your skills, accomplishments, and strengths in a positive manner, and also be prepared to talk about a real weakness and how you minimize it.

- If the interviewer asks you an illegal question, such as your marital status, childcare responsibilities, health status, etc., pleasantly respond, "That's private. Rest assured, I'm prepared to do what it takes to fulfill my job responsibilities."

- Do not lie about your credentials, experience, or current salary. They can be verified.

- Do not ask about salary or benefits. You should already know the pay range for the position.

After the Interview

- Send a thank-you letter to the interviewer (not a card, but a real letter on nice 8-1/2 x 11 stationery). You could call or email, but the interviewer may be too busy to take your call, and an email won't have the impact of seeing a live signature. This little act will serve to remind the interviewer of who you are, give you an opportunity to reemphasize your qualifications and desire to work for the company, and to share a point that you may have forgotten to make during the interview. Send the letter within 24 hours of the interview to make a really good impression. Purchase stationery and stamps ahead of time to avoid delay.

- Don't be anxious about the outcome of the interview. Know that "many are the plans in a man's heart, but it is the LORD's purpose that prevails" (Proverbs 19:21 NIV). Do you really want a job that God doesn't want you to have?

12

Air Travel Etiquette

Despite the frustration of air and ground security procedures, many still brave the world of travel for business and personal reasons. It goes without saying that anytime people come in contact with each other in large or small spaces, there are expectations of what constitutes proper behavior.

- Before you book your ticket, find out what type of plane is scheduled to be used (737, 767, etc.) and confirm the location of your seat on the plane by visiting www .seatguru.com. This site features seat map layouts with comments regarding favorable and unfavorable seats on specific planes. If using a travel agency, be sure to inform them of your seat preferences.

- If you travel regularly, keep a separate set of your essential cosmetics and toiletries packed in your luggage. I use a preprinted checklist of items I must include from toiletries to business cards.

- Before every trip, try to be flexible and to go with the flow. Don't bemoan the extra security requirements. Remember, the airline's goal is to protect you. View all other inconveniences as part of the process of getting to your destination.

- Don't blame the airline staff when flights are delayed or canceled. They are only the messengers of the bad news. Be nice to them, and they just may upgrade your seat—or at least give you an extra snack.

- Pack a generous portion of your favorite snacks and some interesting reading materials just in case you encounter extra delays or arrive at your hotel past restaurant or room service hours.

- Pack as lightly as possible. Plan on basic pants, skirts, or jackets doing double duty. In fact, if you can fit all of your belongings in a carry-on bag (standard size, please), you'll eliminate a lot of frustration. Just keep in mind that if all the overhead bins are filled, you may be forced to check a bag containing a valuable or fragile item that you had planned to keep within your sights.

- Store your carry-on bags as quickly as possible so that you can vacate the aisle during boarding.

- If traveling with a child, be watchful for annoying behavior, such as kicking the seat in front of him, pulling on the headrest, or talking too loudly.

- If you happen to get a Chatty Cathy as a seatmate, gracefully decline further conversation by saying, "I'm going to take a nap" or "I'm going to see if I can finish this book now." You might simply don a pair of headphones. If you didn't bring your own, go ahead and pay the airline charge for them. It's a small price for peace and quiet.

- Consider the passenger behind you when reclining your seat. Do it slowly, making every effort not to cause a spill or other inconvenience.

- If there is an empty seat between you and your seatmate, don't claim all of the extra space. Try to use only half so that she also has the option of using the other half.

- Don't be perturbed because the person with the window seat needs to use the restroom more than once during the flight. If you have an overactive bladder, plan to drink lots of water, or are generally antsy and can't sit still, book an aisle seat (or request one when you check in).

- Men, assist others (especially senior citizens and women) in retrieving heavy carry-on bags from the overhead bins. It's the right thing to do.

- Unless you are about to miss your connection, don't be a pest by making a mad dash to get off the plane. I'm amazed at people who rush for the door almost as soon as the plane touches down, only to spend 30 minutes at the baggage claim waiting for their luggage.

- See the next chapter, "Tipping Tips," for guidelines on tipping from the time you arrive at the airport until you reach your hotel room.

13

Tipping Tips

The word "tip" originated in England and supposedly was an acronym for the phrase "to insure promptness." Although tipping is expected in most situations where someone provides you with a personal service, it is not mandatory. Rather, it is a discretionary kindness that we extend to reward prompt or excellent service. The tipping guide below reflects the appropriate tipping ranges for various services, including those needed or requested when traveling.

Everyday Tipping

Dining Out: Restaurant dining is the most frequent time to demonstrate your tipping savvy. Most people have their own tipping philosophy ranging from nothing to liberal amounts; notwithstanding, a waiter can impact the quality of your dining experience. Those who enhance it should be rewarded; 15 to 20 percent is the norm. A tip is still in order at a buffet if a server brings anything to your table or takes away extra dishes so that you can stuff yourself in comfort; 10 percent of the bill is recommended. This also goes for take-out and home deliveries. If you have a group of six or more, most restaurants will automatically add 15 to 20 percent of the total to the bill. If the service was outstanding, you may add an amount over and above this.

Hairstylists/Barbers: 15 to 20 percent of the service fee. In the past, it was considered in poor taste to tip the owner if he rendered the service. However, with the increasing cost of living, no one's going to be upset to get more money. Of course, if the owner is a member of the elite in his field and considers himself a celebrity, he might be insulted by a meager 20 percent.

Manicurist/Pedicurist: 15 percent of the service fee. If you haven't had a pedicure since Noah closed the door to the Ark, please tip more, and don't be surprised if management tacks on an additional charge for the extra time required for your service.

Massage Therapist: 15 to 20 percent of the service fee.

Tipping When Traveling

There are a myriad of people to tip when you travel and stay in a hotel, so be prepared to fork over the following amounts:

Ground Transportation:

Limo Driver: 15 to 20 percent of the fare. If you are being hosted by an organization, it will most likely be billed for the tip. You may still give the driver a token gratuity of $10 or more or whatever amount you deem appropriate based on the distance to your destination and the amount of assistance the driver provides with your luggage.

Taxi/Airport Shuttle Driver: 15 to 20 percent of the fare. If he provides no assistance whatsoever with your bags, consider the lower end.

Courtesy Shuttle Driver: $2 per person for the ride itself and a minimum of $1 to $2 per bag handled. Also consider any helpful or interesting "tour guide" information he provided on the way to your hotel. If others are accompanying you, tip a flat amount for the entire party based upon the preceding guide— or whatever amount you feel would be fair if you were the driver.

At the Hotel

Doorman: A sincere "thank you" if he simply opens the door; $1 to $2 per bag if he takes them to the front desk. Later during your stay, if he calls or hails a taxi for you, tip him a couple of dollars.

Bellhops: $1 to $2 per bag brought to your room—plus extra if she gets you ice, briefs you on places to go or eat, turns on heater/air conditioner, etc. Give no less than $5 for all services rendered including the bags.

Room Service: An 18 to 20 percent gratuity is always included on the check. Verify it when you sign the bill. This doesn't prevent you from tipping over and above this amount if you so desire.

Hotel Maid: Tip according to the level of the service provided (bed turndown, chocolates on your pillow, extra toiletries, etc.) and the luxury level of the hotel. Put the tip in one of the hotel's envelopes and mark it: "Maid's Tip" (or her name in instances where she has left a card indicating her name). It is best to tip daily. If you wait until the end of your stay, it may be the deserving maid's off day.

Maintenance People: Repairing the TV, air conditioner, or other broken items does not have to be rewarded.

Concierge: (Mispronouncing this word shows lack of travel savvy. Say "kon-cee-airzh.") If this special hotel helper arranges for you to get theater tickets, restaurant reservations, or secures other hard-to-get services, a tip ranging from $5 to $20 is in order, depending on the complexity of your request.

Delivery of special requests (toothbrush, toothpaste, extra towels, or blankets) warrants a reward. Try $1 per item, but never less than $2 for the delivery.

Valet Parking Attendant: Give the person who parks the car a smile and a thank you. If you have an expensive "status" car, you might want to tip the valet who parks your car so that he has incentive to put it in a choice spot. Give the attendant who retrieves your car at least $2 or more. If the valet parking is free, be generous.

- On all tipping occasions, try not to ask for change (if at all possible). Unless you are including the tip on a credit card, be prepared with an appropriate supply of $1, $5, and $10 bills. Have your money ready in a jacket pocket or other handy place when traveling. Ladies, no fumbling in that bottomless pit called your purse.

- Tipping etiquette varies in different countries and cultures. Check a travel guide for your particular destination before you go.

- Always round up to the nearest dollar when computing the tip. It is a good example for others—especially to your children—to see you operate with a spirit of generosity. You'll surely reap the consequences, "for whatever a man sows, that he will also reap" (Galatians 6:7).

- Finally, your tip should be given out of a heart of

gratitude and generosity for excellent service and not from pressure to comply with the social norm. "Each man should give what he has decided in his heart to give, not reluctantly or under compulsion, for God loves a cheerful giver" (2 Corinthians 9:7 NIV).

14

Cross-Cultural Etiquette

With the business world now being one big global community, the workforce being multiethnic, and everyday people traveling regularly outside of their country, it behooves business and nonbusiness travelers to become culturally savvy. To prevent cultural naïveté from sabotaging your business relations or from spoiling your next vacation, arm yourself with the guidelines below.

When Traveling Abroad

- Learn how to say "thank you," "please," "hello," "excuse me," "how much," and other key expressions in the language of the country you are visiting. The natives will appreciate your attempt to fit in. (Don't try to bluff it by making up words as a friend and I did more than 30 years ago when we were trying to find our way back to our hotel in a foreign county. We stopped a gentleman and asked if he knew the way to "el hotello." You can imagine the look he gave us.)

- When in Rome, do as the Romans do. Take care of your cultural homework by consulting books or websites such as www.ExecutivePlanet.com, which explain the customs and behaviors of specific countries. This will help you to avoid making offensive remarks or inappropriate gestures during your interactions.

- Avoid jokes. There's a good chance that the punch line will be totally missed—or considered insulting. (Recently, a friend and I were coaching a fellow from Afghanistan on how to tell American jokes. He was bewildered by what we thought was hilarious.)

- Avoid using slang and jargon. Don't assume everyone automatically knows their real meaning.

- Clearly articulate your words. Remember, when you are in a foreign country, you have an accent.

- Observe proper business card exchange etiquette. For example, in dealing with Asians, offer your card face up toward the recipient with both hands holding the top corners. This humble body language shows respect for the receiver, who will then take some time to study the information on the card. (When I first experienced this, I was slightly perturbed, for I assumed that the recipient was questioning whether I was really the person represented by the card.)

  Also, be aware that when receiving a card from an Asian, you must not desecrate it by immediately putting it into your purse or pocket or scribbling notes on the back—fairly common behavior in the United States. Take a moment to look at it before tucking it away someplace safe.

- Show respect for the local dining fare and do not express distaste or disgust with any dish that is offered. Simply say "no thank you." (Even better, accept a small portion and push it around your plate a few times.)

- Don't point out ways in which your country is superior to the host country. Rather, find something complimentary to say about its history, beauty, or other observable facts. Focus on experiencing the culture as is without judging it.

- Dress appropriately for the culture. Be sure your shoulders are covered (without regard to the temperature) if you plan to visit or tour a religious establishment.

- Don't be offended if someone violates your personal space. In some cultures, people stand very close to each other. For most Americans, our personal space ranges from two to four feet, while most Arabs like to get up close. (Even while shopping in culturally diverse Los Angeles, I've had to ask a person or two to step back after my attempts to create more distance between us failed. I once said, "I'm sorry. I'm slightly claustrophobic and need a little more space here.")

- When you visit another country for business or non-business reasons, you also represent your country. Don't leave others with a picture of an ugly American, Chinese, or other citizen.

15

Your Home Office Image

The U.S. Department of Labor's Bureau of Labor Statistics reports that in 2004 more than 4.5 million people worked at home with a home-based business. As one who hates to drive, I find one of the greatest benefits of working from home is the short commute from my bedroom to the office. Having had a few years' experience in working at home as a full-time writer and speaker, I am well aware of the pleasures and pitfalls of such a flexible environment. To keep professionalism and a spirit of excellence intact, consider the minimum requirements for operating your home office with finesse.

- Have a dedicated business telephone line—no matter how tight your budget. "Mom and Pop" status will be a foregone conclusion when your customers call and are instructed to press "1" for Papa Bear, "2" for Mama Bear, "3" for Goldie Locks, and "4" for the International Jewelry Bazaar. Go ahead and invest in the least expensive phone plan available and stop sabotaging your company's image.

- Work smart. If you tend to lean toward workaholism or your body clock is slightly out of sync with the norm, try to make up for your work-until-the-wee-hours mad-ness by sleeping until you wake up without the aid of an alarm clock. Your trusty answering machine can advise clients that you are unable to take the call and will get back to them promptly.

- Manage personal calls. Your family and friends will most likely assume you are available to chat or run errands 24/7. Why? Because you are at home! You'll have to teach them that you only have limited availability by not engaging in personal calls or other distracting requests for more than a few minutes and only at set times of the day.

- Advise your Federal Express and United Parcel Service drivers as to where to leave (and not leave) your packages.

- While you can now ditch the suits, you'll still want to dress in presentable casual attire to maintain your own professional mind-set. A former boss used to remind the staff that too casual attire yielded too casual an attitude toward work.

- Never flush the toilet while on a call. Enough said.

- Do not allow small children or anyone who sounds unprofessional to answer your business line. If you can't take a call, let the answering machine do its job.

- Be mindful of computer keyboard noise when typing and talking on the phone. If you're taking notes, let others know that you are doing so, lest they think you are distracted and working on something else.

- Before a conference call, silence all other phones in the house, including second lines, fax machines, and cell phones.

- When on a business call, make every effort to shut out environmental noises such as a whirring blender, the doorbell, sirens, ice cream truck music, a lawn mower/leaf blower, barking dogs, yelling children, etc. (One day I was on a radio interview and had gone to great lengths to ensure complete silence, only to have the UPS deliveryman ring the doorbell. I would have been wise to tack a "Do Not Ring Doorbell—Leave Package at the Gate" sign out front.)

- Use your phone's mute button to control noises that are outside of your control.

- Never make the assumption that you can run to the store or post office looking like a hag. You are almost certain to encounter someone you know. Ladies, at a minimum, toss on some lip gloss and a nice casual hat if you're having a bad hair day.

16

Email Etiquette

Email has somewhat changed my personality. Though I am an acknowledged people person, I prefer to communicate with my social and business acquaintances by email because it saves me from having to engage in all the time-consuming preliminaries, required chitchat, and goodbyes. Of course, I'm aware of the downside of this technological convenience in that the human touch is completely eliminated. Further, the potential for miscommunication abounds because the tone of voice cannot always be determined from the written words.

Whether you consider email a curse or a convenience, the guidelines below should help you better mind your manners in this area.

- Do not capitalize all of your words. In the cyber community, this is considered yelling. I know that it's faster to type in all caps, but you won't win any friends with this violation. (The other day, in my haste, I responded to a friend's request in all caps. Her reply was, "Why are you screaming?")

- When replying to an email that has been sent to several people, do not choose "Reply all" unless it is absolutely necessary to disclose the information to everyone.

- If you send a message to a large group of people, do not put all of their email addresses in the "To" or "Cc" field. Instead, respect each person's privacy by putting the addresses in the "Bcc" field. This way, each one will only see her email address on the message. If you leave the "To" field blank, it will show up on the mailing list recipients' computers as To: Undisclosed Recipients. (When you receive an email that discloses all of the recipients' email addresses, do not presume this to be a license to add them to your address book for your future communications. If you desire to contact the group for whatever purpose, kindly ask the sender to forward your message to her email community.)

- Include enough info in the "Subject" field for the recipient to grasp the purpose of the email, for example: "May 14 Conference Budget" versus "Conference" or "Financials for January through March 2008" versus "Reports." Also, including the addressee's name in the subject line is a good attention grabber and might prevent your email from being inadvertently deleted.

- If the subject matter of a series of emails changes, be sure to put the new topic in the "Subject" field, or you will run the risk of having your new issue or concern ignored or missed.

- The fact that email is quick doesn't mean that you should launch right into the message without a salutation ("Mary," "Hello, Joe," "Dear Mr. Brown"). A series of emails sent and received during the same sitting don't need a salutation. Treat them like a phone conversation.

- If you are upset with a sender, go ahead and respond to

the email but save it in the "Drafts" folder. Do not send it until you have gained your composure and prayed about what you've said. Remember, "A soft answer turns away wrath, but a harsh word stirs up anger" (Proverbs 15:1). Also, consider whether it would be wiser to deal with a tense or emotional subject matter via telephone or a face-to-face meeting. Cyber conflicts can become pretty nasty when the parties do not have the benefit of looking into each other's eyes.

- Understand that there is no such thing as a private email. Therefore, do not include anything confidential or improper. (I learned my lesson when a close friend inadvertently forwarded my very confidential email to her list of friends. At least she had the decency to inform me of what she had done and made every effort to do damage control.) Also, be aware at work that some companies monitor employees' email to assure they are not wasting time or disclosing company secrets.

- Know that forwarding off-color jokes, tasteless sayings, or other non-edifying correspondence gives others a glimpse of your character.

- Don't forget to proofread your email just as you would a regular letter or memo. Use the spell check feature, but don't rely upon it completely as it will allow you to use a word out of context as long as it is spelled properly. Remember, when you press "Send," you send your image along with the email.

- Do not be disappointed if you do not receive an immediate response to your email. Everybody's umbilical cord is not attached to the computer. Some people do disconnect and only check email occasionally. If your issue requires a quick response, simply pick up the phone and give the person a call. Notwithstanding, an email recipient should make every effort to respond within 24 hours, just as he would with a phone call.

17

Cell Phone Etiquette

There's probably not a person reading this who has not been irritated by someone's inconsiderate behavior on a cell phone. Cell phone impact may go beyond simple annoyances. Several studies show cell phones are a leading cause of car crashes. It is estimated that cell phone–distracted drivers are four times more likely to be in a car wreck. According to a Harvard University study, cell phones cause more than 200 deaths and half a million injuries each year. Besides physical harm, the emotional frustration caused by thoughtless cell phone users cannot be quantified.

All three pillars of etiquette—consideration, convenience, and common sense—must come into play when handling your cell phone. I hope you'll take heed to the protocols below and become one who uses your cell phone with class.

At Work

If you have small children, dependent parents, or other care-giver responsibilities, everyone will understand your need to be accessible 24/7. Notwithstanding, a ringing phone lessens your productivity and can be annoying to those around you. Consider these guidelines.

- Turn the phone off and only check messages during a break or at selected intervals. Listening to messages is more efficient than answering the phone and engaging in chitchat. Further, you do not want callers to get into the habit of calling you at work for insignificant issues. "Whatever you do, do it heartily, as to the Lord and not to men" (Colossians 3:23). Not only is God watching, but your coworkers are judging your integrity.

- Find a private place to make your cell phone calls. You'll keep your personal matters private and avoid disrupting your coworkers.

- Do not place your phone on the conference table during a meeting—even if it is on vibrate. I've seen phones literally dance on the table. This is unprofessional, rude, and a clear indication that you are one distracted employee.

- Never talk on your cell phone in the restroom. The sound of flushing toilets is tacky.

Nonwork Situations

Cell phone courtesy and consideration are equally important when interacting with others outside your work environment.

- Make every effort to find a private place to make calls, and be mindful of your volume. Don't force those around you to become involuntary participants in your loud conversations.

- When in a public place, let the person you are speaking with know that you are on a cell phone and that the conversation must be kept brief. So what if you have the unlimited minutes plan? Use them in your car.

- Use text messaging if you must exchange information quickly, but be discreet. It is rude to use text messaging to cure your boredom at the dinner table or elsewhere in the company of others.

- Respect and obey restrictions on cell phone use on airplanes and in libraries, theaters, and other public places.

- If you feel that you must answer your phone while in a meeting or during interaction with a friend, client, coworker, or other person, apologize and keep the conversation short.

18

Giving and Receiving Gifts

Do you feel that every month of the year brings an occasion to purchase a gift for somebody in your circle of interaction—be it family, friends, coworkers, in-laws, clients, or employees? Rather than bemoaning all of these special celebrations, remind yourself that "it is more blessed to give than to receive" (Acts 20:35).

Whether for social or business connections, the guidelines below should help you to give and receive with class.

Giving

- Note on your calendar the birthday, anniversary, or other date for every significant person to whom you'd like to give a present or card on his special day. If you use a Personal Digital Assistant (PDA), you can program the dates to appear annually.

- If the gift must be mailed, you should also note on your calendar the date by which you need to send it to ensure timely arrival.

- Keep on hand a supply of generic gifts (and gift bags/tissues) for women and men just in case you forget a birthday or other significant occasion. Such gifts may include movie tickets, lotion/soap gift sets, music CDs, picture frames, or various gift certificates (department stores, spas, restaurant, coffee houses, electronic stores, or other).

- Prepare a holiday shopping budget and shop for Christmas gifts all year long. Make your list and check it twice to be sure that you can really afford to buy something for each person.

- When selecting the gift, consider the recipient's tastes, quirks, or other known preferences. Why give a bottle of wine to a teetotaler or a pound of chocolates to an eternal dieter?

- Be sure to remove the price tag from the gift, even if it is expensive and you want to impress the recipient with your generosity!

- It is not necessary to give the boss a Christmas gift. If the entire staff wants to pitch in for a group gift, then so be it.

- Bosses would be wise to buy individual gifts for their immediate staff or at least treat them to a Christmas luncheon. (I found that hosting the staff at my home was a nice personal touch.)

- For corporate gifts to clients, vendors, etc., find out if your proposed gift will violate any company restrictions (particularly government agencies). Never give cash. Your purpose may be misconstrued.

- Guard against inappropriate gifts to the opposite sex. Avoid anything that can be viewed as intimate, such as loungewear or nighttime apparel. Stick with gift certificates, gift baskets, etc.

- Include a handwritten note with the gift. This has a more personal touch than a preprinted gift card with your name typed on it.

- Don't infer that a gift is more expensive than it really is by putting it in a gift bag from an upscale store. What if the recipient tries to return it?

Receiving

- If you will be receiving several gifts at once, such as for a birthday party, shower, or anniversary celebration, assign someone to keep track of them. This can be done quite easily by having available a pen, some paper, and small self-adhesive stickers. Simply number the stickers (in duplicate) and place one number on the gift and the corresponding number by the person's name (which your tracker will print) on the sheet of paper. This will allow you to thank the person according to the guidelines below.

- You must promptly acknowledge each gift lest the giver conclude that you are ungrateful or did not like it. Keep a supply of thank-you notes on hand and make every effort to get them out within three days of receiving the gift.

The ideal thank-you note expresses your sincere gratitude for the specific gift, how you will use it, and a closing sentiment. For example:

Dear Al and Pam,

Thank you so much for the wonderful flannel sheets you gave us for our anniversary. They will certainly come in handy on those chilly nights here in Los Angeles. We'll think of you each time we use them.

Thanks again for your thoughtfulness.

Love,

Deborah and Darnell

- If you receive a gift that you will not use, remove all evidence of the original giver, rewrap it, and pass it on to someone else later. Unless it is generic, be sure you re-gift it to a person outside of the giver's immediate circle of interaction, if possible.

- No matter how inexpensive or insignificant a gift appears, remember it really is the thought that counts—someone took time to think about you. That is always something to be grateful for.

19

Dressing to Impress

_____

Your appearance speaks volumes about you before you even have a chance to open your mouth. Most people, whether godly or ungodly, will judge you within the first 30 seconds of meeting you. Consider the fact that the prophet Samuel was ready to anoint David's oldest brother, Eliab, king over Israel simply based upon his appearance. God had to set him straight: "The Lord said to Samuel, 'Do not look at his appearance or at his physical stature, because I have refused him. For the Lord does not see as man sees; for man looks at the outward appearance, but the Lord looks at the heart'" (1 Samuel 16:7). Man does indeed look at the outward appearance, and you cannot ignore this reality.

What you wear communicates (or mis-communicates) to the world very important information about you. Since you only get one shot at making a first impression, why not make it one that will serve your best interests? Here are the essentials for women and men on dressing to impress.

Women

- Get the proper fit on your clothing. Clothes that are too short, too tight, or fit improperly in any other way are distracting and confidence robbing. If you are overweight, avoid horizontal and bold patterns. If you are thin, run from vertical stripes. Find a good tailor who will taper or adjust your garments to flatter your body type.

- Know your own color "season" (see www.colorme beautiful.com for guidance) and stick to a color palette that complements your skin tone. While you *can* wear any color, all colors won't flatter you.

- Don't over-accessorize. Swinging earrings, a wig or bangs, a hat, and a busy necklace are simply too much. Less is more for a classy look.

- Dress modestly and tastefully, as in "dress for success, not sex." What exactly would be your motive for exposing your body to the general public?

- Make sure your bras, slips, or other undergarments are never exposed. Buy the necessary strapless bra or a slip with a split to accommodate the cut and style of your outfit. Buy the type of panty hose that prevents a panty line from showing.

- Wear knee-high hosiery only with slacks and extremely long skirts. Otherwise, the tops will show when you sit. Grandma Syndrome!

- Avoid wearing shoes that are lighter than the color of your skirt (or bottom of your dress or slacks). They will draw all attention to your feet. Ignore fashion trends that violate this rule. Your goal is sophistication.

- Remember that it is unprofessional to wear head scarves, wraps, or hats while working in a general business office—unless it's an industry standard to do so (such as in the fashion or advertising industry).

- If in doubt about how to dress at work, adopt the style of the top female executives in your organization.

- Don't let your dress-to-impress efforts drive you into a financial pit. Be an "investment dresser." If you are on a limited budget, invest in a few interchangeable suits in basic colors, such as navy, burgundy, and taupe. Also, buy basic but chic shoes, such as pumps. Rather than buying new clothes each season, update your wardrobe with the latest look in accessories and colorful blouses.

Men

- Invest in at least two suits in a year-round color and fabric. The colors should be interchangeable (navy, brown, taupe, etc.) to maximize the number of wardrobe combinations.

- Avoid wearing the color beige against your face; it makes most skin tones look washed out. French blue is a safe choice for almost everybody.

- Go easy on the cologne. Don't let your scent announce your arrival (same for women).

- Always keep your shoes shined (some women swear that shoes reflect a man's character).

- Keep your nails and nose hairs trimmed.

- If you don't like ironing, remove your clothes immediately from the dryer so wrinkles don't set. (I saw a guy in a restaurant the other day whose shirt was so wrinkled it looked as though it had mini-mountain peaks.)

- Dress properly for the occasion—without your wife or fiancée nagging you to do so. If a jacket and tie are appropriate attire, just wear them and know that this too will pass. You'll get a lot of relational and image mileage for your cooperation.

- When wearing a tie, make sure that it extends to the waist of your pants. Check out www.tie-a-tie.net or www.tieguide.com for instructions on how to tie and care for your ties.

- Coordinate your socks and pants. Make sure your shoes are never lighter than your pants.

- Your socks should be long enough so that no bare skin shows when you are seated. Do not wear socks with sandals; socks are for closed shoes.

- Match your belt and shoes for a polished look.

Men and Women

- Buy clothes of the highest-quality, year-round fabrics (such as lightweight 100 percent wool) that you can afford. Better a few high-quality, interchangeable pieces than a closet full of obviously low-budget items.

- If you are short or overweight, avoid double-breasted jackets. Single-breasted jackets have a more elongating and slimming effect.

- Remember that casual day at your place of employment does not mean you can dress for spring-cleaning, the gym, or the beach. Notwithstanding, the definition and expectations for business casual vary by company and industry. Thus, you must familiarize yourself with the guidelines established by your Human Resources Department. If there isn't an official casual dress code, strive to maintain a polished look with comfortable slacks, cardigans, casual jackets, tops, and so forth. Skip the tennis shoes, white socks, T-shirts, jeans, denim pants or skirts, and spandex tops or bottoms.

- Always keep tiny breath mints available. Place a couple in your jacket pocket for discreet retrieval as needed to freshen your breath. Bad breath is a serious people repellant.

- Know that employers are willing to pay more to a person who looks the part. The inference is that employees who take pride in themselves will take pride in their jobs. If you are self-employed, image is equally important. Look successful and people will seek to be in your circle.

20

Proper Grammar and Diction

During my training at John Robert Powers' finishing school, they taught us that "beauty should be heard as well as seen." I've observed gorgeous, impeccably dressed women ruin their image when they open their mouths. Proper grammar and diction are essential to developing the poise and conversational ease necessary for effective networking, public speaking, and everyday communication. When you know you have a good vocabulary, know how to properly articulate words, and know when to use them, your confidence soars and your voice becomes one of your most valuable assets.

Poor grammar and diction can sabotage your image and cause others to view you as ignorant or uneducated. Interestingly, some of the most articulate people I know are not college graduates, but rather individuals who understand that most people judge your intelligence by how well you speak.

There are an endless number of books written on this subject. If you are challenged in this area, I suggest a visit to your local bookstore, Amazon.com, or other outlets to purchase books (I prefer CDs for the sound advantage) on vocabulary building, grammar, and diction. There are also numerous online resources, such as www.yourdictionary.com with links to other sites offering valuable information. In the meantime, here are some brief exercises to get you started.

Common Grammatical Mistakes

- Using "I" instead of "me." Example, you should say, "John took my wife and me to dinner," not "my wife and I." When trying to decide when to use "I" versus "me," simply eliminate the other person from the statement and say what sounds correct. "John took...I to dinner" (no way!). Similarly, you wouldn't say, "That dog really loved I." So why would you say, "That dog really loved Ted and I"? I think you get the picture now. And, no, you cannot substitute "myself" for "I."

- Using the helping verbs—have, had, or has—with "came, went, ran, etc." For example, it is incorrect to say, "I had came home early that day." Helping verbs must be used with such verbs as "come, gone, and run."

- Improper use of "who" and "which." Use who to refer to people or named animals ("The man who was late" or "I was awakened early by my cat Fluffy, who wants breakfast first thing in the morning") and which for objects and unnamed animals ("The building, which collapsed yesterday, was an eyesore" and "That horse, which is very expensive, is my favorite.")

- Saying "irregardless" (no such word) instead of "regardless."

- Using the word "mute" (unwilling or unable to speak) instead of "moot" (irrelevant, no practical value). Say: "Deciding the color of the carpet became a moot (not mute) point after the fire destroyed the building before it was completed."

Commonly Mispronounced Words

The Word	Say	Don't Say
pronunciation	pro-nun-ciation	pro-noun-ciation
library	li-brary	li-berry
often	off-en	off-ten
government	gov-ern-ment	guv-ment
height	hite	hithe
length	leng-th	lenth
modern	mah-dern	mah-der-ren
athlete	ath-lete	ath-a-lete
diamond	di-a-mond	di-mond
theater	thea-ter	the-a-ter
February	Feb-ru-ary	Feb-u-ary
Realtor	Real-tor	Real-a-tor
hierarchy	higher-archy	high-archy
prescription	pre-scription	per-scription
interesting	in-tresting	in-ter-resting
recognize	rec-og-nize	reconize
Alzheimer's	Alz-heimers	Alt-timers

Poor Articulation

If you have a problem with poor articulation, a few sessions with a speech therapist will be money well spent. They have really helped me slow my pace. I used to get so excited about my subject matter that I'd leave my hearers in the dust. For now, practice reading out loud from a book or newspaper. Read word by word and exaggerate each sound with special emphasis on the word endings.

You may also find it helpful to repeat the list of words below several times making the "ing," "t," and "d" ending sharp in every word:

- singing, and, shopping, and, going, and, getting, and, giving, and, fighting, and, flying, and, trying, and, testing, and, marketing, and, mimicking.

  Insert your own frequently used words that end in "ing" for an exercise more tailored to your needs.

- that, and, cat, and, rat, and, rest, and, told, and, just, and, list, and, coast, and, nut, and, pocket, and, let, and, about, and, test, and, bold, and, cold

You may wish to develop a list of words that you commonly mispronounce or find difficult to articulate, especially words used in your profession. Write them out and be sure to confirm the correct pronunciation before you begin your drill. Practice makes perfect, and you don't want to practice perfectly wrong. Repeat each word at least five times in a row, saying "and" in between each word.

21

Entertaining at Home

My hat is off to anyone who takes the time to entertain others in their home these days, in which most people are challenged to find the time to meet family, friends, and acquaintances for a relaxed gathering even in a restaurant. But in the early days of the New Testament church, hospitality was an indispensable virtue. In fact, it was a prerequisite for one to be a bishop or elder: "He must enjoy having guests in his home" (Titus 1:8 NLT). Showing hospitality is still the hallmark of a child of God. If you have decided to take the plunge, follow the guidelines below for a rewarding experience.

- Decide on the purpose of the gathering and what you'd like to achieve in hosting an event. It is not to show off your house (or is it?), so resist the temptation to embark upon a remodeling project.

- Decide on the type of event: an informal gathering, formal dinner party, or other.

- Determine how much you want to spend on the entire event so that you can tailor your menu and invitation list to your means.

- Decide who will and will not be invited: couples only,

friends with children, singles, immediate family only, etc.

- Extend the invitation in a timely manner (one month before the event, minimum). The type of invitation lets your guests know the type of party you are planning.

- Except for informal events, in which guests are notified via phone or special "evites" (online invitations), invitations should be mailed even if you have secured a verbal attendance commitment. If extending the invitation by phone, give as much detail as possible so that your guest can make a quality decision to accept or reject. "Delisa, I'm giving Darnell a surprise birthday party next month on Saturday, the fifteenth, at 6:00 p.m. here at our home. I'd like for you and Kelvin to join us. I'm inviting 15 couples or so." Don't put the guest in a no-win position by asking, "What are you guys doing on Saturday night?" After all, they could be free but may not desire to attend your function. Again, give the details up front. By the way, if you are planning to ask guests to bring a covered dish (potluck style), let them know at the time you extend the invitation—not after they accept.

- Don't over-invite. While a few people (even those who RSVP'd but forgot to cancel) may not show, you must plan for adequate seating for all. There are few party inconveniences worse than having to stand with a plate in one hand and trying to cut a chicken breast with the other. A few days before the party (and before you buy final food supplies), check with guests who haven't responded—just in case their invitations got lost in the mail.

- If you are considering an outdoor event, plan for unexpected weather changes. Also, advise the guests to wear hats, wraps, or appropriate clothing suitable for the environmental conditions.

- Don't try to do everything yourself. Secure the services of a personable student, relative, neighbor, or other person to assist with last-minute errands, chores, etc.

- Remember that you set the tone for the party, so get into a fun mood no matter what frustrations you have encountered. Get dressed in plenty of time and be ready to greet early arrivals (or at least have an official greeter ready to do so for the early birds).

- If you plan to serve buffet style, arrange the food in a logical order: meats, veggies/sides, salads with dressing options in bowls with spoons (no bottles on the table), breads, butter, and condiments. Consider having the main entrées dispensed by a server in order to control those guests whose eyes are larger than their stomachs.

- Introduce people to each other. If you see someone sitting alone, introduce him to a chatty friend who can carry on a conversation with a stop sign.

- Don't show sadness, disappointment, or anger if somebody breaks something or spills punch on the carpet or furniture. Plan ahead to only serve non-stain-type drinks (no red punch, etc.) if you have light-colored carpet. If you are the responsible clumsy guest, offer to pay for any damage you caused.

- If you decide to assign seating, carefully consider the personalities and common interests of the people who will sit beside each other.

- Ending the party will often test your patience and gra-ciousness. Some latecomers may feel they need to make up the time. If you have hired help, arrange with them to clear the food away at a preset time. Now, if you're having a great time and have no plans for the next day, you may tolerate lingering guests for as long as you'd like—while also considering other people who reside in the household. My husband has been known to exit a gathering and retire to the bedroom without cere-mony. If you are absolutely ready for all to call it a night, simply say (with a big smile), "Thank you all so much for coming and making this event what it was. I really appreciate it. I want to wish all of you a safe trip home." Go and stand by the door and hug everybody goodbye.

22

Houseguest Guidelines

The Shunammite woman in the Old Testament was the epitome of hospitality. Not satisfied with merely hosting the prophet Elisha and his servant, Gehazi, for dinner on a regular basis, she convinced her husband that they should add a room to their home to accommodate the duo during their frequent visits to the area (2 Kings 4:8-11). Elisha and Gehazi were obviously good guests whose presence added value to the household. Notwithstanding, sharing living space with even the best of friends can often create tension. Following the guidelines below for those extended stays should ensure a rewarding and stress-free time of fun and fellowship.

Tips for the Host/Hostess

- Don't go overboard in sprucing up the house; clean it but don't redecorate.

- Find out what foods/snacks your guests like and dislike, and then make every effort to accommodate their dietary preferences.

- Get enough rest the night before so that you're not tired and irritable when the guests arrive.

- Determine prior to their visit if your guests would prefer to rest or explore the local attractions/movies, but don't plan every minute. Leave time for lounging and great conversation.

- Clear a space in the closet for their clothes.

- Have a set of common toiletries (toothbrush, toothpaste, mouthwash, etc.) on hand in case the guests forgot theirs.

- Give first-time guests a tour of the relevant sections of your home and explain all house rules up front (answering phones, setting security alarms, letting pets in/out, turning off television, recycling, etc.). Explaining these rules to them later as each violation occurs can be irritating and unwelcoming.

- Let them know if any special or diet foods are off limits, such as Grandma's favorite sponge cake or your weight loss protein bars. Keeping them out of sight is the best strategy where possible.

- Place a few amenities in the guest rooms, such as mints, tissues, etc.

- On the last day of their visit, explain what to do with used linens (do nothing, stuff in pillow case, etc.).

Tips for the Houseguest

- To show appreciation for your host's hospitality, bring a small gift that she (or they) will use or enjoy; for example, movie tickets, gourmet coffee, herbal teas, etc. Avoid gifts that might create work for the host. Unless you know that your host has a green thumb, do not give live plants, herb gardens, etc.

- Bring your own toiletries (toothpaste, shampoo, etc.). Unless you are assigned to your own private bath, keep them in your room. Do not spread them out in the common bathroom.

- Respect your host's property. Do not snoop in the closets or cabinets. (I heard of one woman who filled her medicine cabinet with marbles so she would know when a guest was snooping!) Do not place wet glasses on wood furniture; use a coaster. Do not put your feet on the couch or cocktail table. Is this how you behave at home? If so, then ignore the host's offer to "make yourself at home."

- It's okay to inform the host that you are on a special diet and require specific foods. It is a good idea to bring your own such foods if you are serious about losing weight. I'm an eternal dieter and always bring low-calorie food with me when we stay with our close friends. Unfortunately, I usually succumb to the fattening fare and end up bringing most of my "rabbit food" back home! It's now a standing joke.

- Do not make long-distance calls from the host's telephone without permission. Use a calling card when possible if you do not have a cell phone or cannot get reception in the area.

- Do not invite someone else over for a visit without the host's permission.

- Do not give your personally invited guests a tour of the house.

- Since you're saving on accommodations, pick up the dinner tab at least once during your stay. Offer to pay for the gas if the host takes you sightseeing or does extensive driving.

- Strive to be a low-maintenance guest. Don't expect your host to prepare every meal or to entertain you the entire time of your visit.

- Dress appropriately for the household. Avoid wearing revealing clothing in the presence of the host or hostess of the opposite sex.

- Always clean up behind yourself. Help clear the table, wash dishes, etc.

- Keep your room tidy at all times. The host may decide to invite other guests over.

- Follow the host's instructions on handling bed linen at the end of your visit.

- Always send a handwritten thank-you note within a day or so. Keep a supply of thank-you cards on hand for this purpose. An email is fine for really close friends that you visit overnight on a regular basis.

23

Dating Protocol

For most singles, the ritual of dating is a precarious under-taking. This is an arena where consideration and common sense must be exercised with all diligence. Who knows? You just may find your life partner—or not. Notwithstanding, the protocols below are a must if you plan to survive the dating scene.

Guidelines for Women

- If you were not introduced to your date by a mutual acquaintance or other trusted person, consider meeting him at a restaurant or other public place for your first date. Never give your address to a complete stranger.

- As a safety measure, always leave a note in your apartment or home with the name of the date and the planned meeting place. Also, let a friend or family member know of your plans. Unfortunately, you cannot be too trusting these days.

- Don't approach the date as an opportunity to evaluate a man's suitability as a life partner. Why not just decide to have a great time and look for ways to learn more about men in general?

- Make every effort to be on time. Tardiness may be his biggest pet peeve (same for the men).

- Don't dress seductively and then become offended when your date makes sexual advances. Why advertise a product that is not available?

- Be a lady. Don't use profanity or talk too loudly.

- Practice good dining etiquette (see chapter 4 on "Confident Dining"). This also goes for men.

- Don't order the most expensive entrée on the menu just because he's treating. Choose an entrée in the mid-price range.

- Don't be a Chatty Cathy. Listen with interest to what he says. On the other hand, don't try to squeeze him for a detailed psychological, relational, or financial history of his life on the first date. There will be plenty of time for that if things progress to the next level. Rather, stick with safe questions about his hobbies, job, travel, and other interests.

- Don't complain about the "dogs" that you've dated in the past. Assume he is different until he proves otherwise.

- Laugh. Be a fun date.

- If a red flag of emotional instability, financial irresponsibility, uncontrollable temper, or other negative character trait manifests, don't rationalize it away out of your desperation for a relationship. Run!

Guidelines for Men

- Show up as promised. Only cowards stand up women. (I accepted my first date with my wonderful husband after another man stood me up. His loss, my gain!)

- No matter how liberated, assertive, or accomplished your date is, treat her like a lady and extend the traditional courtesies of opening her door, walking on the traffic or dangerous side of the street, and showing her respect in every way.

- Pick up the tab on the first date (unless she insists otherwise). Don't think that doing so entitles you to anything more than a wonderful evening in the presence of a lovely lady. Of course, if you both decide to split the bill, so be it.

- Do not promise to call if you know you have no intentions of doing so. Just thank her for accompanying you on the date (even if you had a rotten time) and say goodbye.

- Don't be offended if she refuses to give you her personal information. She doesn't know yet if you are Jack the Ripper or Willie the Wonderful.

- If after several dates (at least three or four), she has made no gesture toward reciprocating (even in a small way, such as buying the popcorn at the theater), consider if you have a gold digger on your hands. Just be careful not to jump to this conclusion too quickly, especially if she has hinted that she is having financial difficulties. Rather, start engaging in no-cost activities, such as a walk in the park, stroll on the beach, board games played at home, etc.

- If you determine that you are incompatible, cut your losses. Tell her so and move on.

24

Gym Etiquette

On one of my rare visits to my gym recently, I was most annoyed by a woman who sat at a particular machine and carried on a lengthy conversation with someone between sets. How inconsiderate! I was once again reminded of the three pillars of etiquette: consideration, convenience, and common sense. I saw none of them come into play at that moment.

Although most gyms will post their general guidelines, participants don't always follow them. At a minimum, the following need to be observed.

- Silence your cell phone.

- Learn to use the equipment properly to preserve its effectiveness and to keep from aggravating others with banging noises, etc.

- Be mindful of people who are waiting to use the equipment. If you're in slow motion, step aside and let Speedy Gonzales complete his routine in between your sets.

- Follow the other rules of the gym regarding proper attire, time limits on treadmills, bikes, etc.

- Wipe off equipment after use. No one wants to share your perspiration. If your gym doesn't provide cloths for this purpose, grab a few paper towels from the restroom or locker room, or bring a towel from home.

- Do not disturb others by singing along with your headphone music.

- Put free weights and other portable equipment back where they belong.

- Bring your water and towel to each workout station. Don't annoy or interrupt others by leaving them three or four stations behind.

- Men, resist ogling the women exercisers. Women, dress appropriately. Enough said.

- Try to do challenging lifts and exercises without grunting loudly. Does this really help?

- Even though you plan to work up a good sweat, be mindful of your hygiene prior to starting your workout.

- If you need help with the equipment, ask the gym personnel. Try to minimize the interruption of other guests as much as possible.

- If you run into an old friend, keep your little reunion private. Others have no need to hear the details of your conversation.

25

Church Etiquette

Church attendance is something every believer should make a priority, if possible. The apostle Paul encourages us not to forsake "the assembling of ourselves together" (Hebrews 10:25). Church is the one place where everyone should be accepted "as is" without regard to his pedigree, financial status, or other factors. Notwithstanding, there is a standard of etiquette that should be observed in order to honor God and the dignity of His house. Further, you must respect the rights of others to attend services without distraction or discomfort.

Because etiquette is the customary rules for conduct within a select group or society, certain protocols and customs may vary by denomination. The guidelines below, however, transcend sectarian differences and will help you to be a considerate, savvy churchgoer.

- Dress appropriately for the house of God. Avoid revealing outfits that may distract the opposite sex; for example, low-cut tops, high skirt splits, tight pants... get the picture?

- Refrain from sitting on the front row if you are wearing a skirt that rises above your knees when you sit—unless you have a scarf or handkerchief to cover your legs. This can be a great distraction to the minister.

- Generally, do not consume food or beverages in the worship facility or chew gum. (However, I understand that these are acceptable practices at more informal churches. Just be mindful of your environment.)

- If you must enter or leave the service while it is in progress: 1) avoid using the center aisle, if possible; 2) do not cross in front of the pulpit or podium where the pastor or anyone else is speaking; and 3) do not enter or exit during Scripture reading or prayer.

- If your child must accompany you to the adult service (versus attending the nursery or children's service), sit near the rear of the church—close to the aisle—so that you can make a quick (and perhaps temporary) exit if Little Johnny's behavior dictates it. Excuse yourself promptly. Don't frustrate others by tuning out his noise.

- "As you enter the house of God, keep your ears open and your mouth shut" (Ecclesiastes 5:1 NLT)! The house of God is a place for worship and reverence. Refrain from engaging in loud, jovial conversations.

- Obey the ushers' instructions. Do not insist on sitting in "your" special seat just because you gave enough in the building fund drive to pay for it. If asked to march to the offering table, as is the custom in some smaller churches, don't inconvenience others by staying in your seat and requiring them to step over you to exit the row.

- As in other public places, silence your cell phone.

- If you decide to join another church, do so gracefully.

Officially advise your current pastor of your plans via a short letter. If possible, call or meet in person. Whatever your reason for leaving, resist making negative remarks about the pastor or the ministry to others. God just might decide to send you back there later.

26

Wedding Guest Etiquette

Since there are many books available on protocols to be followed by the bride, groom, and wedding party, I'll limit this chapter to coaching you, the wedding guest, on the guidelines by which to govern your behavior.

- RSVP promptly—whether you plan to attend or not.

- If the invitation to the reception doesn't say "and guest" next to your name, don't write in your desired guest's name, do not ask to bring a guest (the reception cost is usually based on a head count), and for goodness' sake do not show up with an uninvited guest.

- Refrain from wearing an all-white outfit. Give the bride the respect and sole right to this color for her day.

- Dress appropriately for the wedding venue. If it's held in a church, avoid backless and other revealing outfits.

- Arrive early. Everyone will be nervous enough without having to deal with someone interrupting the processional.

- Don't hinder the effectiveness of the official photographer by taking pictures when he is doing so. Ask him to signal all the amateurs when it's okay to snap away.

- When going through the receiving line, feel free to congratulate the couple on their union or even say "Congratulations" to the groom, but keep in mind that it is considered poor taste to congratulate the bride, for it infers that you are applauding her for successfully snaring a man. Just say, "Best wishes for a happy life" or, even more simply, "Best wishes."

- If you did not RSVP, don't crash the reception. If you are a close friend, advise the wedding organizer of your plight. There just may be a cancellation that will allow you to attend after all.

- Do not switch the place cards at your designated table at the reception banquet in order to sit next to familiar friends or family. Honor the arrangement that has been established by the bride and groom.

- Be on your best behavior. Be patient and flow with the long delay in starting the wedding or reception and all other annoyances and inconveniences.

- Don't tell stories of the bride or groom's escapades with the opposite sex. That's all history now.

- Schedule a huge block of time to attend the entire wedding and reception. Try to remain until the cake has been cut.

- If there is a buffet, don't cut the line. Use this time to make new acquaintances.

- Even if you cannot attend, but have been extended a formal invitation, you should buy a gift for the happy couple.

- Use the gift registry as a guideline for what the couple

desires; however, buy early if you're on a budget as the less expensive items go fast. Also, feel free to buy a more affordable, meaningful, or useful gift not on the registry (such as neutral-colored bath towels, nice 5x7 picture frames, etc.).

- If you decide to recycle a gift that was given to you for your wedding or other occasion, be sure to remove all evidence that it was given to you and rewrap it to fit the occasion.

- Put a card or note inside your wrapped gift so that if the wedding card gets lost, the couple will still know whom to thank.

- Enclose a gift receipt where possible so that the couple can exchange the gift if they desire.

- Consider delivering your gift prior to the wedding and save the couple the trouble of trying to get all those presents home.

- Honor the couple's requests for cash gifts. Although considered tacky or rude by popular etiquette mavens, such requests are becoming commonplace and generally accepted. To boot, financial institutions as well as the U.S. Department of Housing and Urban Development are now offering bridal down payment registries which allow guests to contribute to a couple's purchase of a home. Let's face it, if the bride or groom has already established a household or the couple must merge two residences, the last thing they need is more stuff. So let's give some leeway here and remind ourselves again of one of the guiding principles of etiquette: common sense. Notwithstanding, don't allow such requests to intimidate you into giving more than you desire or can afford. Scripture cautions every one to "give as he purposes in his heart, not grudgingly or of necessity; for God loves a cheerful giver" (2 Corinthians 9:7).

- Honor the couple's request for "no gifts." (Once a bride very ungraciously rebuffed me for buying a gift after I accompanied my elderly mother [as her officially invited guest] to the wedding. The bride exclaimed, "I said no presents! Now I'm going to have to send you a thank-you note." Well, excuse me for not looking at the invitation!)

27

Funeral Etiquette

Every culture has some type of ceremony that acknowledges a person's death and allows family and friends to officially mourn their loss. Following the essential protocols below will assure that your behavior is considerate, dignified, and encouraging to the bereaved.

- Dress conservatively for the funeral service. While it is not necessary to wear black, choose attire that will show dignity and respect for the bereaved and the occasion.

- Arrive on time. If you're late, try to be seated as inconspicuously as possible.

- If you are asked—or decide—to make remarks, please obey the stated time limits. Don't ramble on and on.

- Be reverent and respectful of the deceased even if you are not familiar with him and are only attending the funeral because of your relationship with one of his relatives. (I have seen people thoughtlessly and with total disregard for the family engage in loud laughter and jovial handshaking with old acquaintances only steps away from the casket as the family exited the church.)

- Do not take pictures of the deceased. Let the pictures

on the funeral program suffice for your memories or ask the family for a photo later.

- If you attend the traditional postfuneral lunch or reception, it's okay to encourage the bereaved to express their feelings and thoughts.

- Do not pry about the details or cause of death. Just listen attentively if the bereaved should decide to talk about it.

- Do not make negative or insensitive comments regarding the appearance of the corpse.

- When expressing your condolences, resist platitudes and clichés such as:

  > "She's in a better place."

  > "Life must go on."

  > "God decided to pluck a special flower, so He took her."

  > "Well, he lived a full life." (Please note that love does not diminish with age. Even if the deceased lived to be 150, the bereaved will most likely wish that the death had been delayed.)

- Do not make matters worse for the bereaved with such statements as "If only Beth hadn't _____, she'd be alive today." Remember that your goal is to comfort, not to find ways to place blame. This is exactly what Job's well-meaning friends did who came to support him in his grief. Initially they gave him the gift of their presence. "They sat down with him on the ground seven days and seven nights, and no one spoke a word to him, for they saw that his grief was very great" (Job 2:13). How commendable! After some time, however, they felt they needed to justify why Job had lost his children, his property, and his health. So they blamed him for his woes and argued with him that surely he had sinned. It's no wonder that in exasperation he exclaimed, "Miserable comforters are you all!" (Job 16:2). Don't be a miserable comforter.

- If you are wondering, "Then what should I say?" try one of the simple statements below:

    "I'm so sorry."

    "Susie was a fine woman and a good friend. I'll miss her."

    "It was good to know Ted."

    It is also appropriate to relate a kindness or favor that the deceased extended to you.

- The bereaved may respond to condolences by saying, "Thanks for coming," "He talked about you often," or any other expression of appreciation. Let graciousness rule.

28

Ten Tips for Teens

The manners and protocols that apply to adults also apply to teens. But, just in case you are a teen and decided to skip all other sections of this book, here are ten social behaviors you'll want to be sensitive to, especially as they relate to this unique stage of your life.

- Show some personality; start by smiling. Yes, being a teen is tough, but don't make the world pay for your frustration by being surly, detached, or sullen. Be different. Be personable.

- Remember the birthdays of key adults in your life and at least send them a card. If you can't afford a small gift, offer to perform a service for them (raking leaves, washing the car, etc.). They'll be grateful for the attention.

- Respond with enthusiasm and gratitude (as in "Thank you very much") for any gift or kindness you receive. You are not automatically entitled to other people's money (even parents and relatives) or favors.

- Think twice and consider your future before you get a tattoo or a permanent carving in a conspicuous place on your body. You just may run for a political office one day or become a corporate president.

- Respect adults by calling them "Mr." or "Ms."/"Mrs." rather than by their first name unless they give you permission to do otherwise.

- Honor your teachers in every way. Don't join your classmates in disrespecting them. Trust me, you'll stick out in those teachers' minds.

- Girls, don't jeopardize your reputation or your safety by wearing outfits that emphasize or reveal your breasts and buttocks and leave nothing to a boy's imagination. Boys, underwear is not to be exposed ever (as in low-riding pants). That's why it's called "under" wear. Most adults will assume you are associated with the wrong crowd. Summer employers find such attire undesirable. Remember that man looks at the outward appearance.

- Use your "indoors" voice in the mall and other enclosed areas. Save yelling for your favorite sports team and other outdoor events.

- Be "bi-social." Slurp, smack, put your elbows on the table, and break all the rules of dining etiquette if you must when you are at the local burger stand with your friends, but when eating with your parents and other adults, please observe the rules of dining etiquette (see chapter 4 on "Confident Dining"). They'll be impressed and may even reward you for it.

- Don't engage in text messaging when you are dining or socializing with your family or other adults just because you are bored. Ask questions about their old fogy childhood and bring them up to speed on what's considered cool today.

29

Social Blunders

We are all bound to make a social faux pas at some point in our existence; however, the blunders listed below are common and should be avoided at all cost.

- Asking a woman when her baby is due and then having her inform you that she's not pregnant.

  Instead: Unless you know for sure that a woman is expecting, never assume that her expanded waistline means she's pregnant. Make no reference to it.

- Exclaiming to someone in the presence of others, "Wow, you've lost a lot of weight!" It's not news and it implies she was huge before.

  Instead: Simply say, "You look great." Even here, use wisdom. If she is accompanied by an obese friend, keep the compliment low key.

- Saying "sir" or "ma'am" to someone based on their appearance only to discover that he or she is of the opposite sex. One day I was in a department store and I said, "Thank you, ma'am…I mean, sir…I mean, ma'am…" (I wanted to vanish!)

Instead: No need to make a gender distinction. Just "Thank you so much" will do.

- Asking an older gentleman if his date is his daughter, only to learn that she's his new wife. Asking a woman if a man is her son, when in fact he's her husband, is even worse!

  Instead: Don't quiz people about their relationship to the person accompanying them. Let them volunteer the information.

- Telling a friend, "I'll see you at Nick's party on Saturday" and having him ask, "What party?"

  Instead: Never assume that mutual friends always invite each other to every function. Do not discuss an invitation with anyone else in the same circle of interaction. This goes for invites from the boss, pastor, or anyone else.

- Making negative comments about someone only to discover that you are talking to his close relative.

  Instead: If you can't say something nice...stuff it!

- Saying "old folks" in the presence of the elderly when relating a story or incident.

  Instead: Just keep living...and see if one day you'd like to be referred to this way. "Senior citizen" is the socially acceptable term.

- Using the term "Colored" or "Negro" when talking to or referring to Blacks.

  Instead: Keep up with changing times. To be safe, use the same term that news commentators use when referring to an ethnic group.

- Expressing the results of your successful bargaining by saying, "I 'Jewed' them down." This is offensive to Jewish people.

  Instead: "I drove a hard bargain and won."

- Telling a joke (even a clean one) that pokes fun of a particular ethnic group.

  Instead: Steer clear of ethnic jokes! They can derail your career for sure.

- At a social gathering, asking about the absent spouse and then learning that the couple has divorced.

  Instead: Hey, you can't always keep up with the details of people's lives. Simply say, "I'm sorry to hear that."

Controlling the Damage

Although offending someone was not your intention, it is no less painful to the person. Because most people are not assertive enough to say, "I'm offended by that," you'll have to be socially smart and spiritually discerning enough to detect a problem and to make an effort to mitigate the damage.

- Be alert to a sudden change in someone's attitude or abrupt departure during your conversation or interaction.

- Inquire if you have said anything offensive. "Did I say something that hurt your feelings or embarrassed you?" Or, if you have a hint of what might have upset the person, "Did I upset you by asking you to let me finish my point?"

- Apologize and state your good intention. Scripture admonishes us to always take the initiative in restoring harmony: "If you are offering your gift at the altar and there remember that your brother has something against you, leave your gift there in front of the altar. First go and be reconciled to your brother; then come and offer your gift" (Matthew 5:23-24 NIV).

30

Popular Pet Peeves

I solicited input from my email community, friends, family, and others regarding their pet peeves—annoying behavior of others that drives them up the wall. Rather than elaborating on their responses, I'll just present them and remind you that a socially smart person strives to avoid behavior that irritates others or makes them uncomfortable.

The question presented to respondents was "What is your biggest social or professional pet peeve?" The most popular responses are listed below.

Everyday Interactions

- The number one annoyance? "Cell phone users who engage in loud, personal conversations in a public place" (planes, grocery stores, movies, elevators, gyms, etc.).

- "Retail clerks or grocery checkers who are mean, indifferent, or refuse to say 'hello' when you approach their register. How do these people get hired to work with the public when they have no personality?"

- "Retail workers who openly complain about some aspect of their job (shift schedule, long hours, coworkers, etc.) in the presence of customers."

- "When I'm in the checkout line at the market with only one or two items and the person in front of me has a full basket but doesn't offer to let me go ahead of her."

- "When a person in front of me holds up the checkout line rummaging for correct change."

- "Indecisive people—especially when they take forever to give the waiter their order."

- "People who need a breath mint and respond 'No, thank you' when you offer them one."

- "People who slurp, smack, or suck their teeth when eating."

- "When people bang their silverware against their plate, shake the ice in their classes before drinking, or make any other noises while dining."

- "People who swoosh water in their mouth when dining with others. Cleaning braces is no excuse. This should be done in private."

- "The sound of someone chewing ice."

- "The sound of someone eating during our telephone conversation."

- "People who pop gum or chew it loudly."

- "Cashiers or salespersons who talk on their cell phones and do not even bother to acknowledge your presence when ringing up your purchase."

- "Men who undress women with their eyes by staring them up and down. I'm especially irritated by it if he is with another woman. How humiliating is that for her?"

- "Women with a bad attitude. Must I or the whole world be punished for their painful history?"

- "When somebody borrows my money and then can't be found after the date that he promised to repay it."

- "When I offer someone some candy, gum, bottled water, etc. and they take an extra supply."

- "Friends who want to split the restaurant tab equally when they have ordered everything except the kitchen sink and I've only had soup. How convenient for them."

- "People who interrupt someone when having a conversation or in conflict. Is their brain really not capable of retaining a thought until the other person finishes his?"

- "When I graciously allow another driver to go ahead of me and he doesn't acknowledge my kindness by waving back."

- "When I'm dining out and someone who gets introduced to me while I'm eating wants to shake my hand. Has he considered the fact I may not want to share his germs? How about a simple 'hello' or a nod?"

- "When a person calls my house and asks, 'Who is this?' without identifying herself first."

- "Thin people who complain about their weight in the presence of an overweight person."

- "People who judge others by their size."

- "When somebody calls me 'honey,' 'dear,' or 'sweetie.' I consider it a put-down."

- "People who stare at me. What's up with that?"

- "People who stand too close and violate my personal space. I need at least four or five feet unless we're intimate."

- "People who chew gum constantly—even quietly—in church or other public place, like a cow chewing cud."

- "People who interrupt your conversation with another person without saying 'Excuse me.' "
- "People who exaggerate."
- "People who have strong opinions on subjects about which they know very little and have no valid support."
- "Argumentative people."
- "A car passenger who knows I'm going in the wrong direction and tells me after I realize I'm lost."
- "When a little unruly kid keeps stepping on the back of my shoes when I'm waiting in line at an amusement park, grocery store, or other place—and his parent seems totally oblivious to his actions."
- "When I invite a select group to play a round of golf, and one of them who finds he must cancel invites a substitute player without checking with me first. Big no-no! Golfing is as much about the camaraderie of the players as it is the game itself. Substitutions should be approved by the person who secured the tee time."

At the Office

- "Coworkers who talk too loudly in the office."
- "Employees who goof-off and engage in extended personal conversations."
- "A manager who implements a new policy for everybody when there is only one offender of the existing policy whom he is too chicken to confront."
- "People who bark orders, make demands, and treat everybody as their servants—and forget to say 'please' or 'thank you.' "

- "So-called professionals who tend to overeat at company-sponsored buffet luncheons/dinners or people who ask the waiter to bring them an extra serving of a dish at a banquet. Why don't they eat what's offered and pig out in the privacy of their homes?"

- "A person who brags about...anything."

- "Managers who reprimand subordinates publicly."

- "Being put on a speaker phone without permission."

Epilogue

onfidence is rooted in knowledge. In presenting the information in the foregoing chapters, I attempted to provide you with the tools to act with confidence in key social and professional situations. While space did not permit me to engage in expanded discussions of the various topics, I hope the tips, guidelines, and suggestions have given you a foundation for becoming a model of graciousness and social savvy. The more you practice them, the more easily you will sail through every social interaction without confusion or intimidation. Further, when you make a commitment to civility and graciousness in every aspect of your life, people will be inspired by your example. When you decide to govern all of your actions by the three principles of etiquette—consideration, convenience, and common sense—your relationships improve. Flexibility and understanding become a natural response even in dealing with difficult people.

Supreme Court Justice Clarence Thomas said, "Good manners will open doors that the best education cannot." Yes, learning and engaging in the proper behavior is a *good* thing that has great earthly rewards. Treating others the way you want to be treated is the *right* thing to do, and the rewards are eternal.

Bibliography

Books:

Bates, Karen, and Karen Hudson. *The New Basic Black* (rev. ed.). New York, NY: Broadway Books, 2005.

Bixler, Susan, and Nancy Nix-Rice. *The New Professional Image* (2nd. ed.). Holbrook, MA: Adams Media Corporation, 2005.

Fox, Sue. *Etiquette for Dummies* (2nd. ed.). Hoboken, NJ: Wiley Publishing, Inc., 2007.

Freeman, James M. *Manners and Customs of the Bible.* South Plainfield, NJ: Bridge Publishing, Inc., 1972.

Mitchell, Mary. *The Complete Idiot's Guide to Etiquette* (3rd. ed.). Indianapolis, IN: Alpha Books, 2004.

Platz, Ann, and Susan Wales. *Social Graces.* Eugene, OR: Harvest House Publishers, 1999.

Whitmore, Jacqueline. *Business Class.* New York, NY: St. Martin's Press, 2005.

Websites:

www.bremercommunications.com

www.etiquetteexpert.com

www.protocolprofessionals.com

www.executiveplanet.com

www.elaineswann.com

Deborah Smith Pegues

30 Days to Taming Your Tongue

Who hasn't struggled at times with foot-in-mouth disease? Certified behavioral consultant Deborah Smith Pegues uses short stories, anecdotes, soul-searching questions, and scripturally based personal affirmations in this 30-day devotional that is tongue-and-life-changing.

30 Days to Taming Your Finances

Sharing her expertise as a public accountant and behavioral consultant, Deborah Smith Pegues sheds light on the emotional and practical side of organizing, spending, saving, and sharing finances wisely and the freedom this brings to life.

Forgive, Let Go, and Live

If you've been wounded by another, this book will empower you to find joy, freedom, and peace as you let go of your desire to avenge the wrong and make a commitment to release the offender from his debt.

Emergency Prayers

Deborah Smith Pegues offers you a 9-1-1 prayerbook for life's many circumstances and crises. Brief, immediate, and heartfelt, these prayers bring God's Word to the forefront of your mind as you seek guidance, comfort, and strength.

30 Days to a Stronger, More Confident You

You can understand and overcome the fears that limit you. And you can build the confidence you need to reach your personal and professional goals. Through Scripture-based principles, heart-searching personal challenges, and healing prayers and affirmations, you'll discover the path to a more successful you.

About the Author

Deborah Smith Pegues, a former Fortune 500 VP, is an experienced certified public accountant, a Bible teacher, a speaker, a certified behavioral consultant specializing in understanding personality temperaments, and the author of *30 Days to Taming Your Tongue, 30 Days to Taming Your Finances, 30 Days to Taming Your Stress, Emergency Prayers,* and *Supreme Confidence.* She and her husband, Darnell, make their home in California.